SPARTACUS 2.υ

HOW SLAVERY STARTED, STILL CONTINUES AND CAN BE ENDED

Mikael Nordfors MD

Spartacus 2.0

How slavery started, still continues and can be ended

Mikael Nordfors MD

Illustrations by Arnstein Myggland, own photos and paintings + free material from Internet. The book cover is from private photos.

Publisher: BoD – Books on Demand, Stockholm, Sweden
Printing: BoD – Books on Demand, Norderstedt, Germany

ISBN: 978-91-7969-205-6

Table of contents:

Introduction:

This is the second, edited version of the book from November 2019, "Demosocracy, The Solution to The Political Dilemma" The initial co-writer, Loke Hagberg asked me to not be a co-writer anymore because of personal reasons. I thank him deeply for his support to help creating this book from the start and for his support in proof-reading and giving constructive feedback and ideas. I have added some updated info relevant to the Covid 10 crisis, near death experiences and the psychological consequences of slavery that were not present in the previous edition.

The purpose of this book is to help to create a world free from slavery, tyranny, and oppression.

The root of this problem has to do with the institution of slavery that was a byproduct of the change from the hunter and gatherer society to the large-scale agricultural society many thousand years ago. This change had the advantage of us being able to feed more people but had the disadvantage to make us leave the way of life we have been adapted to for millions of years. The result was a society called" the conquering culture" dominated by people with power addiction, fighting and manipulating each other in their insatiable quest for world dominance, with slavery, oppression, wars, and limited freedom of expression as a consequence.

The invention of democracy and its implementation has limited some of the worst consequences of this phenomenon, but there is still a long way to go in order to create an oppression-free society.

With the development of the Internet, traveling and modern media, the world has become a "global village", where everyone can contact everyone else directly. On the other hand, the economic power over the world has been more and more centralized, and we are seeing the development into more and more of the "one percent society", where only the super-rich ripe the fruits of the increased productivity.

This book postulates that a new organizational model and political system named Demosocracy can become the antidote to the corrupted power hierarchies that currently govern our world. Demos means people, Sophus means wisdom and Kratia means power in the Ancient Greek language. Demosocracy creates wise governance by combining the hands-on experience and control of the crowd with the knowledge and wisdom of the experts (who in this system are not corrupt).

This invention has hopefully solved the ancient old debate from Plato's" the state" if the experts (Sophus) or the people (Demos), shall rule(Kratia). The solution is not either or, but both, in a harmonious co-operation. This is called Demosocracy, and I am sure that Socrates would have agreed about this, if he had been alive today.

In Demosocracy, everyone has equal access to decision making and can decide for themselves when they want to take an active part in politics, company decisions and decisions in their local surroundings or choose not to - with the help of modern technology, assisted by the best experts available.

There will be maximal transparency and no power positions to fight about. However, implementing Demosocracy is not only about introducing a new voting system and a new way to organize politics, law, science and businesses. It is also a new way of thinking and relating, and has great therapeutic implications for mankind that I hope it can lead us to a freer society with a decentralized, human-friendly and high-tech new garden of Eden as result.

About the author:

Mikael Nordfors is the father of Liquid Democracy and Demosocracy and the first person in the world who created a party and a software for Liquid Democracy. Nordfors is also a medical doctor, author, pianist and composer. He is a co-author of the International Bestseller Hypericum & Depression and the producer/composer/of four Music CD: s.

He has been advising many high-level officials and governments like former President Michail Gorbachev, the United Nations, the Labor Party in Great Britain, the Democracy Collaborative and the Federal Election Committee in the US, President Benazir Bhutto of Pakistan, the Patriarch of the Greek Orthodox Church, and the Swedish, Canadian and Finnish Governments.

Today, many of us feel like we are powerless to shape our own reality. We are stuck in this anonymous machine we call society. We have our daily duties, carry them out and sometimes have spare-time. A lot of time is spent hunting for meaning, meaningful relations, meaningful activities – and they are all marketed in a way that always keeps you hunting, it can never stop, you can never be complete. Wherever you go, you will see the faces of unhappy slaves, a wage-slave, working in a factory, an opinion-slave, working in science or media, with the choice of freely expressing themselves or losing their work and reputation, a medicine slave, having to prescribe poisonous medicines that do not heal in a system kidnapped by the medical industry, a political-slave, having to adapt to the viewpoints to what is popular, in order to get re-elected, a fashion-slave, an upper class-slave, having to confirm to all the stiff manners of the upper class, or get rejected, a company-slave, doing all the right things in order to make a career, a teacher-slave, having to teach the children to become slaves, a

consumer-slave, needing to have money in order to survive...

Even the masters are slaves in a way. The business CEO is a slave under the pressure from the shareholders and the board, and board members and owner's slaves of the stiff demands from the international competition. When you walk in the street in a major western city, you see all these slaves stressing around, hardly noticing their surroundings in the hunt to be" good enough", and this never happens, just like in the myth of King Sisyphus, who was forced to roll an immense boulder up a hill only for it to roll down when it nears the top, repeating this action for eternity.

What is a slave?

Encyclopedia Britannica (1) defines slavery as" A condition in which one human being was owned by another. A slave was considered by law as property, or chattel, and was deprived of most of the rights ordinarily held by free persons."

Even if formal slavery was abolished in most countries of the western world more than 100 years ago, the repercussions of this terrible invention are still widespread among us, and we all suffer greatly from the culture, religious believes and economic system created by slavery.

A slave has some basic characteristics:

1. A slave is owned by someone else.

This means that they are not free. They cannot do whatever they like without asking for permission first. They are neither responsible, nor in charge of their own life.

2. A slave is a commodity, not a human being with a spirit.

The wage-slave is a commodity of their employer, the consumer-slave a commodity for the market, the medical-slave a commodity to the health system, and in the end, the citizen is a commodity of the state.

This mentality destroys our perception of ourselves and our relationships. We start to view everyone as a commodity supposed to be used, instead of real person with their own needs and values, independent of us. Our children and our partner will be our property instead of fellow beings, our friends are stepping stones in order to make a career, or possible customers for a multi-level marketing system.

In the family movie" Madagascar" this is very well illustrated in the scene where the Lion Alex comes to the jungle for the first time, whereupon his friends from the Zoo suddenly are transformed from friends to" steaks".

This mentality has poisoned our society and is sometimes masked under the term" a professional attitude" In the working situation as lawyers, doctors, banking employees etc., we are not supposed to show any feelings, neither engage emotionally in our relationships with co-workers and customers. The result is that we spend most of our day in some sort of emotional vacuum, which can be one of the main causes for the widespread prevalence of depression insomnia and anxiety in our society.

3. Slaves have no right of respect, or human rights.

The owner of a slave can do whatever they like to their property. They can punish them, rape them and even kill them without any repercussions, just as they can throw out their sofa any time. The only reason to care for them is that they are of value to the owner and can be used. If the owner tortures their slaves too much or don't give them food, they will not be good workers, and in the end make the owner lose money. just as their sofa will not look beautiful and be comfortable to sit inside when they receive guests if they do not take care of it. The commodities have no value in themselves and can be replaced at any time.

4. Slaves have a price tag.

Slaves always carry a price tag and can be sold and bought on the market any time.

In our culture, most of us have price tags, and can be bought and sold on the market any time. We have sexual price tags on the sexual market and price tags on the employment market. We compete fiercely with our fellow beings in order to raise our price tags.

This price tag also reflects our self-perception and makes us unconsciously divide ourselves in different status-realms and takes away the true self-confidence from everyone. We identify ourselves with our price tag, and the slaves with a high price tag often becomes arrogant, and the ones with a low-price tag suffers from bad self-confidence. The result is the creation of a false ego, where we identify ourselves with our role as commodity instead of our true nature.

It does not matter whether the price tag is 10 dollars or a 100 million dollars, a slave is still a slave.

Natural hierarchy will exist as long as there are scarce resources and supply and demand thus govern those prices. The point is that the perception should primarily not focus on the price and instead on intrinsic value.

5. Slaves never work enough

As the masters wants to get maximum profit out of their commodity, the slaves are almost always forced to work much more than they want and what is healthy for their mind, body and spirit. In special cases (where the rights of the workers are plenty) they keep wages down to the minimum level for maximum productivity.

6. Slaves have no intrinsic value and are not supposed to stand up for themselves.

As a consequence of the greed of their masters, their slaves are newer considered to be good enough.

This is cemented in the Mosaic religions in the story of original sin. When you are punished capriciously, you are primed to believe that you are arbitrarily guilty as well.

It is of utter importance for the masters to take away the self confidence from their property, in order to make them obey, and think more of the wishes of their masters, than on their own needs.

7. Slaves are not equal to free humans and are supposed to kneel down to their masters.

You have to behave differently to you masters than to your fellow slaves, don't look into their eyes, not be too friendly etc.

8. Slaves can be sold any time

Slaves have no right to personal relationships. Children can be separated from their mothers, siblings from each other and husbands from wives.

In tribal societies, the tribe always stay together, and in most cases, the extended families live together for the rest of their life. These strong personal bonds are one of the main foundations of human well-being, and the main reason that poor people in the third world, who have a more tribal lifestyle often are and look much happier. Major epidemic studies have found much lesser prevalence of psychiatric diseases in third world countries, with a more preserved extended family structure than in the west (2).

The new killer in the western world is loneliness, and lack of meaningful human relationships. Now, many are sitting alone in their one-room flats, watching the TV series" friends", or playing computer games instead of meeting real friends.

Families are often separated over many continents, and friend bonds are often not as strong as the tribal family bonds. You often choose friends because of common interests, or that they fulfill your expectations of a friend. If you or your friend have a crisis, is sick, or have a bad day, you are less likely to not walk out of the relationship if he/she is a family member compared to if you have no familiar ties.

Nowadays, the young people spend so much time with their computers, that they don't even have time to meet each other and have sex. The sexual debut age has increased with more than one year in the US (3).

One of the reasons that the royal families and the upper class often had many divorces and bad marital relationship might be that they were most of the time not brought up by their real parents, but by slaves (nannies), who were exchangeable, so that their parents didn't have to bother taking care of children.

In the movie The King's Speech from 2010(4), King George VI only met his parents once a week in his childhood in a scene that resembles a military parade more than a close relationship. The same is now happening to us in the western world, where our children more and more are brought up by exchangeable wage slaves in impersonal day-care institutions and schools. Living alone with a frustrated lonely mother in a small flat is also not a good alternative for a child, compared to being taken care of by an extended family in a tribal community. The same is true for the elderly.

I once visited a lecture by the famous clown-doctor Patch Adams, where he asked the audience:" How many of you would like to spend your last days in a nursing home?"

No-one raised their hands. Then he asked the obvious question:" Why do we then have nursing homes?"

We believe there is a strong relationship between the repercussions of slavery, and the fatal epidemic of loneliness and alienation in the western world.

9. Slaves are not Supposed to be Happy

In many cities in the western world, it is considered as a sign of mental illness if you look happy. If a slave looks too happy, the master might think he has been lazy and have not performed his tasks properly.

10. Slaves are not supposed to have Love

Slaves does not have time for love. To love also means taking care of your own and the other persons needs and comfort. That is a luxury slaves cannot afford. They can also be separated ant time from their loved ones by being sold, which means investing in love and strong personal relationships is futile.

11. Slaves have no right to govern their own Sexuality.

Prostitution and trafficking are consequences of slavery. The Masters, who are often incapable of having mutual loving relationships (or have them to preserve power within the family) compensates this by the use sexual slaves or prostitution.

12. The ultimate slaves are the (non-human) Animals. (5)

Before slavery, the total biomass of wild animals on our planet was ca 400 million tons.

Now it is:

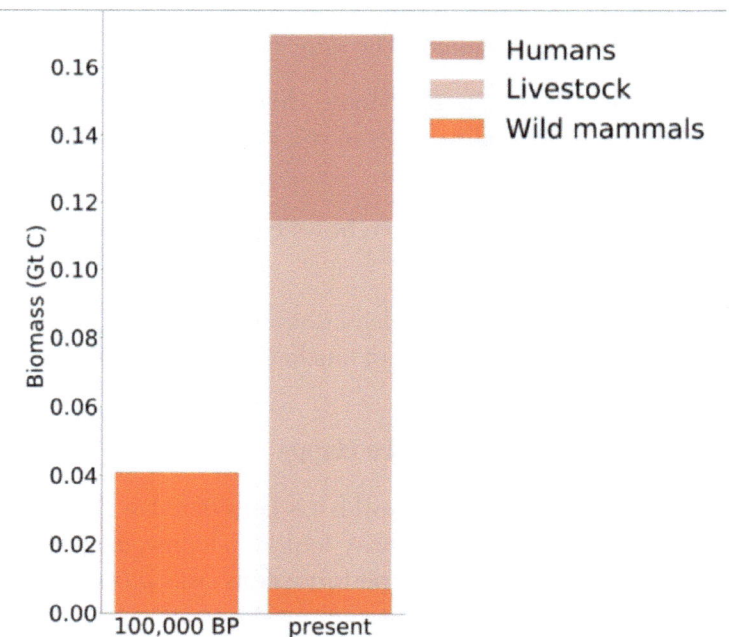

Fig. S5. The impact of human civilization on the biomass of mammals.
The biomass of wild mammals, livestock (dominated by cattle) and humans before human civilization and at present. Values are based on estimates presented in detail in the relevant sections for humans and livestock, wild mammals and pre-human biomass.

600 million tons of the animals are cattle and livestock, 350 million tons are human beings and 20 million tons are wild animals. Soon, there will be no free wild life on our planet if this development continues.

The Master Demon

The result of the slave mentality is that we all will end up with some kind of faceless ghost-like entity in our subconsciousness, that constantly whispers to ourselves:" You are not good enough"," You don't work hard enough"," Nobody cares about you"," You are not allowed to do what you ally want" etc.

This demon is the result of many years of programming from our slave dominated society, and is not as present in tribal people as in the western world. We believe this is the main reason they are happier, although they most of the time have much lower material standard. In this book, we will teach you some techniques on how to exorcize this ghost.

Summary:

The slavery system has made us lose our self-respect and freedom, made us identify ourselves and our fellow beings with our price tag and our position in society, instead with our true spiritual self. This has taken away very much of our natural love for life and our fellow human beings. We become spiritual zombies, remotely controlled by someone we hardly not even know and feel powerless without any inherent value, separated from our relatives and fellow beings. We feel helpless, not in control, and that is one of the main causes for the growing rates of depression and the galloping use of psychiatric medications and illegal drugs in the present" civilized" world.

It also is the main reason for wars, poverty, inequality, starvation in spite of massive increases in production capacity and the emptiness many feel inside that they try to compensate with consumption, entertainment and porno.

John Lennon describes it on the spot in the lyrics of his song

" A Working-Class Hero"

"As soon as you're born, they make you feel small

By giving you no time instead of it all
Till the pain is so big you feel nothing at all
A working-class hero is something to be
A working-class hero is something to be

They hurt you at home and they hit you at school
They hate you if you're clever and they despise a fool
Till you're so fucking crazy you can't follow their rules

A working-class hero is something to be
When they've tortured and scared you for twenty odd years
Then they expect you to pick a career
When you can't really function, you're so full of fear

A working-class hero is something to be
A working-class hero is something to be

Keep you doped with religion and sex and TV
And you think you're so clever and classless and free
But you're still fucking peasants as far as I can see

A working-class hero is something to be
A working-class hero is something to be

There's room at the top they are telling you still
But first you must learn how to smile as you kill
If you want to be like the folks on the hill

A working-class hero is something to be
A working-class hero is something to be

If you want to be a hero well just follow me
If you want to be a hero well just follow me"

This picture might make you anxious, maybe you disagree, maybe you even like life this way – no matter what, you can have it better, there is another society possible – one where we cooperate and co-shape reality in a meaningful way that makes us feel complete every day, where we can have more spare-time and spend it on things which are actually meaningful. We can end slavery.

How? You may ask, perhaps you do not believe it.

It is rather easy really, but to diagnose the problems of the current state, we need to analyze how we got here...

References chapter 1:
1: https://www.britannica.com/search?query=slavery
2: Psychol Med Monogr Suppl. 1992;20:1-97. Schizophrenia: manifestations, incidence and course in different cultures. A World Health Organization ten-country study. Jablensky A1, Sartorius N, Ernberg G, Anker M, Korten A, Cooper JE, Day R, Bertelsen A.
3:https://www.theguardian.com/commentisfree/2018/nov/21/millennials-sex-stressed-young people worry
4: https://en.wikipedia.org/wiki/The_King%27s_Speech
5:https://www.pnas.org/content/pnas/suppl/2018/07/13/1711842115.DC1/1711842115.sapp.pdf

Illustrations:
https://upload.wikimedia.org/wikipedia/commons/b/b2/New_office.jpg

https://www.pnas.org/content/pnas/suppl/2018/07/13/1711842115.DC1/1711842115.sapp.pdf

The Garden of Eden:

Animals that are governed by their instincts experience behavior's that are necessary for survival as pleasurable and comfortable, while that which constitutes a danger to them is perceived as unpleasant.

A lion does not need to muster a lot of self-discipline to go out hunting. A squirrel does not need a five-year plan to gather nuts. And people need not to be forced to go out in the forest in order to gather berries and hunt.

Moose hunting in northern Sweden is a veritable festival. During the autumn weekends, the forests are crowded by mushroom and berry pickers who enjoy filling their baskets even though it is really much simpler to buy the berries in a store.

Almost all human recreational activities are related to hiking, hunting, gathering of food or making us attractive to God/gods and the opposite sex.

The hunter and collectors still live strong among us, but now we have transformed hunting to sports, and collecting to shopping.

Maybe it's our time as hunters and gatherers, which in the Bible is symbolized by the Garden of Eden - a time when we still lived well on what nature had to offer and our work to survive did not take so much time that we have no time to play, sing, enjoy and rest.

According to new findings, our hunter-gatherer times were a real golden age when we only needed to work approximately four hours per day with relatively pleasurable activities such as hunting and collecting and could spend the rest of the time devoted to rest and social activities. (1)

Even today there are a few people who live like this in some remote islands or in the inaccessible jungles of South America, Africa and Asia. These people live in harmony with nature (until their existence is threatened by multinational forest companies, huge dams or highway facilities), they are often very loving towards their children and have enormous reverence and respect for both their ancestors and nature itself.

Social organization is characterized by small, autonomous units where everyone knows each other and live in an "extended family" with much warmth, closeness, and community. Private property is an unfamiliar concept and the tribe members share collectively both to life's joys and its difficulties. There is often a certain hierarchy, with a chief and a shaman ("medicine man") in the organization's peak, but these positions are dependent on the tribal members' support to in order to maintain their status.

There are a number of laws and taboos, but these are not formalized in writing and lives in an oral tradition, just as the tribe's history, myths, legends about ancestors and creation stories.

There is no indication that the war in the modern sense occurred in the hunters' and gatherers era. The graves that have been found from the pre-agricultural times contains far fewer cracked skulls and other signs of violent death, than subsequent burial places. (1)

The Emergence of the Conqueror Culture:

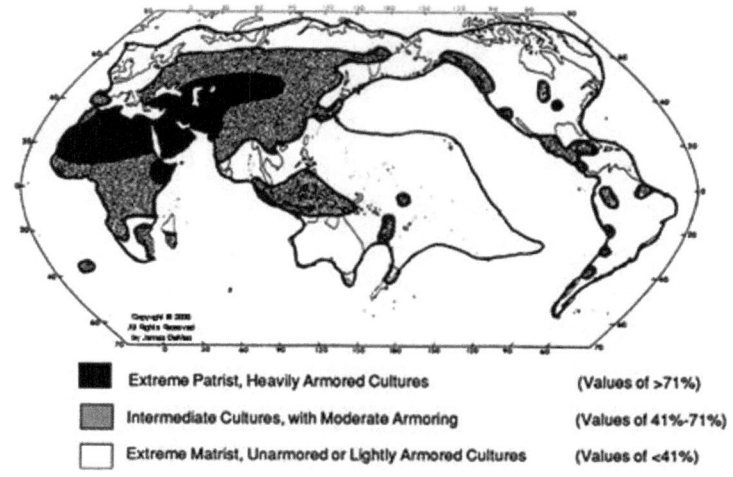

■ Extreme Patrist, Heavily Armored Cultures		(Values of >71%)
▨ Intermediate Cultures, with Moderate Armoring		(Values of 41%-71%)
□ Extreme Matrist, Unarmored or Lightly Armored Cultures		(Values of <41%)

5000-10000 years ago, there was a huge upheaval in people's living conditions.

Essentially there were two inventions that were behind this, namely the agricultural revolution and the written language.

Perhaps this is how it could have happened: Starvation and deprivation due to poor hunting or gathering, food shortages and increased competition for land forced led to a new kind of organization. It was found that the availability of food increased if you started to actively plant crop.

This new organization enabled us to supply food for many more people in the same area. It also meant that we left the kind of life we had lived for millions of years.

Instead of following our instincts and desires in order to live in harmony with nature, we had to walk behind a plow twelve hours a day, reaping, threshing, building houses and storage buildings, clear land, mine coal and metals. We had to cultivate "character" and "self-discipline". We needed the work ethic that could force us up before dawn and keep us going until we fell into bed at night. Religion incorporated these ideals into our belief systems, and the only way to avoid hell and end up in a better place was to obey and believe.

The height of self-discipline and mortification stood for saints. Relaxation and normal human desires were seen as immoral and destructive principles and representations of "the devil".

With the concept of private property and money came a tremendous increase in the number of conquests, power struggles, conflicts and war. We were able to expand our territory and our assets by attacking nearby communities. A warrior class emerged, which could also be used to protect the new ruling class privileges against its own subjects. The upper class could thus live a life of parties, hunting and gathering while property-less slaves had to work hard in order to survive - a pattern that has not changed significantly during the latest millenniums in our history.

War became a profitable business. A large army usually beats a small one, which meant we were forced to organize ourselves in bigger and bigger unities in order to survive. Almost all small, tribal communities were conquered and enslaved, until the major kingdoms covered almost the entire planet. The only surviving natural tribal societies existed in places not yet accessible to the conquering culture in remote places like the Amazons and distant islands of the South Pacific etc.

In his book" Saharasia" (2), Professor James DeMeo from the United States do a cross-cultural review and mapping of data from over 1000 different human cultures. An early period of generally peaceful social conditions is documented in the prehistory of humanity, but with a large shift towards patriarchal-authoritarian and violent social conditions in the Sahara region following a major climate shift from fertile grasslands to harsh desert conditions at ca. 5000-4000 BC. Then living conditions and cultures changed drastically. This also coincides with the introduction of agriculture in ancient Turkey / Mesopotamia about 10,000 years ago. Large epochs of cultural diffusion are also presented on maps showing how violent patriarchal authoritarian, sex-repressive and child-abusive behaviors spread from their Sahar-Asia origins to almost every corner of the world. It presents previously unknown geographical patterns in dozens of different human behaviors, beliefs, and social institutions representative of human violence and war-like aggression, such as slavery, caste systems, genital mutilation, and women's oppression.

Written language was invented and developed to facilitate information transfer in the growing kingdoms and principalities. Written law and religion would maintain order in a society where the oral tradition was no longer the key.

Use of aggressive, proselytizing of religions such as Christianity and Islam were promoted, in which, despite its founder's sermons on love, respect and tolerance had conquest and obedience as the first item on the program. Religion's main message was blind obedience and submission to God, King, and Country. In the name of religion, a number of restrictions on sexuality and bodily pleasures also were inflicted. The Mosaic religions removed all remnants about reincarnation, which was the common belief in many earlier cultures like the Celts, Egypt, Hindus, Buddhists, and many native people and introduced the concept of a heaven for the obedient and an eternal hell for the disobedient.

Frustrated males with low self-confidence, full of guilt were easier to enslave and force to go to war, than happy, self-confident and loving people. Men were not allowed to settle down and start a family before they had been fighting as soldiers.

The women should at the contrary marry as soon as possible so that they could breed many children that could make the state even more powerful by breeding more warriors and slaves. Women's sexuality was denied, and punished severely if it still showed up. The witch hunts in Europe during the 17th century had a clear mood of repressed sexuality and women's power, forces so strong that only cruel torture and painful death was enough to keep them curbed.

The religions also preached strict upbringing of the children with corporal punishment and hard work. The "black pedagogy" as the psychoanalyst Alice Miller (3) described it, had as its purpose to train children into obedient workers, warriors and birth mothers. This was achieved not without problems, as mental health problems, neuroses and personality disorders were sometimes the result of too much self-denial and discipline.

Inability to feel empathy and a certain callousness, however, could show to be really useful features on the way up in their careers, and for the soldier, who's mission it was to realize the conquering ideology on the battlefield, insensitivity, and cruelty were desirable virtues.

Almost all peaceful and humane tribes fell victim to the dominating conqueror cultures, where the Romans, the Greek, the Vikings, the Mongols, the Arabs, and the Anglo-Sachsian culture are among the most successful ones.

This conquering culture has been spreading like a big cultural cancer growth over Planet Earth in the latest millennia and turned everything into a living hell for most of the population.

In Christian countries the Catholic church, and later also the Protestant church made an outspoken campaign against all remnants of the old nature religions and also the traditional knowledge of herbs and various manual, spiritual and mental healing methods who were deeply prevalent in the folk tradition and often managed and passed down orally from generation to generation.

Wise women and men with knowledge of natural therapies were accused of collaborating with the devil, and was burnt at the stake, after enduring torture and inhuman interrogation methods. In many countries, there is a non-broken continuation from the inquisition to the present medical authorities, who continue the tradition of persecuting independent minds and healers.

References chapter 2:

1.A History of Sweden, from Ice Age to Our Age, Herman Lindqvist, Norstedts, ISBN: 978-91-1-301455-5

2: Saharasia: The 4000 BCE Origins of Child Abuse, Sex-Repression, Warfare and Social Violence, In the Deserts of the Old-World Paperback – 20 May 2011 by James DeMeo

3: https://en.wikipedia.org/wiki/Alice_Miller_(psychologist)

Illustrations:

1. https://commons.wikimedia.org/wiki/File:Jan_Brueghel_de_Oude_ en_Peter_Paul_Rubens_Het_aards_paradijs_met_de_zondeval_van _Adam_en_Eva.jpg

2. Picture from "Saharasia" by James DeMeo.

The Consequences of Slavery

Helplessness:

According to the American psychologist Martin Seligman, there is no feeling that is more harmful to the human psyche than the experience of powerlessness and helplessness. (1) Almost everyone has at some time experienced how it feels to be exposed to a large disappointment or loss. If we cannot find any way out of the painful and hopeless situation, a depressive reaction will be triggered. We become sad, lose appetite, we have sleeping problem and become apathetic and anxious. Often, we become too edgy and aggressive. If it gets really severe, we can get caught up in thoughts of suicide.

This reaction is not specific to humans. Virtually all animal species, from monkeys, birds and dogs to earthworms and cockroaches, can exhibit these symptoms.

In its most extreme form, it enters into a kind of coma, with a cessation of both mental and physical functions. Eventually, this leads to death, either by suicide or because life simply stops by itself.

In our organism there is a kind of built-in self-destruct mechanism, similar to the secret agent's cyanide capsule that he takes if caught by the enemy in order to avoid being tortured and risk to reveal classified information to the enemy.

This destruction mechanism is activated by severe mental and physical trauma and is designed to save us and our fellow species from unnecessary suffering when we are in a hopeless situation. Examples of such situations, severe illness and pain, old age, becoming an outcast, or abandoned by the "herd" and immediate threats to life itself, or the quality of life in which all hope of a dignified life seems to be lost.

This inherited suicide mechanism is mediated through changes in the metabolism of certain so-called neurotransmitters in the brain, such as endorphins, serotonin, norepinephrine and dopamine.

This mechanism also affects the hormonal metabolism and the parasympathetic nervous system and can in many animals lead to bradycardia (Slow heartbeat), cardiac arrest and sudden death. Some examples from nature:

Sea birds affected by oil spills often die spontaneously, although the cleaners succeeded to wash them clean and they are not sick or injured otherwise. Animals placed in captivity to be transported to the Zoo often dies spontaneously (roughly 50%), although they have access to food and all sorts of important supplies. But there are also plenty of examples from the world of humans. According to the neurologist, psychiatrist and concentration camp survivor, Victor Frankl the common denominator for those who managed to survive captivity in war prison and concentration camps was the ability to keep hope alive, while those who fell victim to depression and despair died in a much greater extent. (2)

In the animal world (and probably also the case in the dawn of mankind), the depressive reaction and the spontaneous extinction of the life forces of sick and outcast individuals helped the species survive by relieving the herd from the burden of carrying responsibility for very old, sick and abnormal individuals. It also relieved the herd from the burden of having to kill their own relatives, thereby weakening the social bonds in the herd. In our modern society however, we are no longer biologically dependent on the weaker individuals destroying themselves. A human being, which is based on the insight that each individual being is unique and that every life has a special meaning, see nothing "Natural" in the fact that just the most sensitive and most vulnerable are sacrificed in favor of some fascistic "survival of the fittest" ideal.

To instead try to give someone who is desperate, hope again is a genuinely human, and basically civilized act, as we in today's modern society have drastically changed our living conditions.
We have also increasingly become exposed to a variety of situations that can trigger the depressive reflex. Physical illness, old age, loss of loved ones, experiences of powerlessness in the home or at work, fear of unemployment and economic setbacks, loneliness and social failures - the list goes on. Our role in society is no longer obvious in the same way. We have to form our identity ourselves. This is a big responsibility. The world seems to have grown, and although we are in some ways has become more involved because of the increased availability of information and the media's ability to roll into the whole planet in our living room, so does also our impotence because we are exposed to a variety of disasters and global problems that we cannot intervene with very much.
For many, this creates enormous feelings of guilt, and if you cannot find any way to break this feeling of powerlessness it make take you into depression and apathy.
Increased mobility in today's society brings with it a high divorce rate. Permanent separations, break-ups and dissolution of the smaller social network, we managed to spin around us brings feelings of isolation and alienation, of not being a full member of the "herd" All these things activate our depressive reflexes.

Nowadays, we manage to keep our old people alive longer than ever, but we can often not offer them any meaningful role in society. Instead they are often seen upon as a burden to society costing lots of money for health-care, social support measures and pensions. Old age is now often associated with depression and despair rather than with the wisdom and respect that a long life with many important life experiences should provide.

Unfortunately, often care homes and hospital routines take precedence over all individual concerns in the present health care system. All the old are treated exactly the same, regardless of personalities, background, interests and habits.

Many studies show that if older people, which have largely lost the ability to take care of themselves, may be able to influence their own situation they often become dramatically better. It can be about choosing health care and housing, doctors, bank account or lunch menu, the color of the nightgown or where to go on a promenade. The choices must be tailored to the individual, but it is always important even if it appears to cover only small things. Those who perceive themselves to be master of their lives are simply healthier and more active.

So although the standard of living (until recently) has steadily risen over the past half century and we have enjoyed increasing freedom and opportunity to realize ourselves, we become increasingly depressed. But depression can take various expressions. Many adolescents respond with aggression and destructive behavior as a reaction to the feeling of powerlessness and hopelessness, while the elderly and especially women become depressed and passivated.

Man is in childhood, one of the most helpless animals on the planet. Few other animals have such a long period of development before they can stand on its own and fend for themselves. Up in in the twenties, most of us are in different ways depending on parents, teachers and other adults, and therefore we must submit to their discretion, mood and ideas. This makes mankind also one of the most psychologically vulnerable of all species. It places very high demands on the human parents.

Research shows that so-called "learned helplessness" is one of the most important factors of both physical and mental illness in both humans and animals.

If children are constantly forced to experience that in no way can affect their situation whatever they do, the risk that they will develop various anxiety and depression states will increase significantly.

The day when Peter Pan died

Peter Pan is the rebellious boy, who refuses to grow up, and he is continuously fighting with his arch enemy Captain Hook.

He is also forever young. There are many similar stories children literature, another one is Pippi Longstocking who refuses to be controlled by Ms. Prysselius, the school teacher that wanted Pippi Longstocking to become "normal" child that could attend her school.

In the movie Hook, Peter Pan is an adult, who forgot that he once was Peter Pan and could fly, and he is brought back to Neverland in order to wake up from this adult zombie life on order to get truly alive again.

Every child is born a rebellion that wants to be alive, full with life spirit and enthusiasm. In the beginning, we all protested when we were subjected to the carrot and the whip of our masters, but in the end, most of us lost our soul and gave up, and became obedient slaves, controlled by our inner master demon. At that moment, we also lost our soul and our dignity, and from then on, we started looking upon people with a soul with envy and fear. For some people, this transformation happened at the age of five, for other when they were fifteen.

It is the sad moment, when your soul fell asleep, and your artificial robot ego took over.

For a few rare people, this never happened. These people can sometimes survive as artists, authors, musicians or in other creative fields.

Being alive today's society of today is a great challenge, and you will almost certainly be subject to lots of criticism and disdain from "normal" people, telling you that you are mad, crazy, ill-behaved etc. etc. Our world is full of Ms. Prysselius minded people.

Therefore, these people often prefer to be left alone if they cannot find other alive people to spend their time with.

Some of them are only partly alive. This condition can bring lots of suffering and increases the risk for suicide and depression. They are not dead enough to fit in society, but not strong enough to resist it. This can lead to depression, inner conflicts and many psychiatric problems. Whatever they do will be wrong. If they follow society, they will feel like they have sold out themselves and feel bad. If the follow their inner mission and soul, they will feel guilty because they are not good enough slaves. Many of these people can end up in mental hospitals.

A majority of the population instead become "Normopaths" in order to survive.

These people have managed to bury their soil deep enough, so that they totally have forgotten that it once existed. They can live seemingly normal lives and behave well, but create a toxic environment for every child and every person that is still alive.

Their mission in life is to kill all spontaneous life, so that they don't have to be painfully reminded any more about how dead they are. This is symbolized in the legend of Dracula, where the bite of the vampire transforms a person into someone who is a living dead, who in turn can turn other humans into vampires like himself by biting them and drinking their blood.

Vampires in real life have the following personality traits:

- They are "perfect" and criticizes everyone who is not "perfect" enough. Sometimes they don't do this openly, because they are well behaved, but you can certainly feel it on their energy and gestures.

- They are always in control, and also wants to control everyone else, unless they are confronted by an "authority" with a higher ranking in the pecking order. Then they transform into an obedient slave.

- They are pecking order dependent, which means they always try to figure out if you are higher or lower in the pecking order and thereafter adjusts their behavior accordingly.

- There is no spontaneity or creativity.

- They have no humor

- They never admit doing mistakes or apologizes for wrongdoings, as they are always "perfect".

When you meet someone like this, we recommend you to go somewhere else. It is not healthy to stay around such people.

It is actually proven that it is dangerous for your health to hang out with these people. In the 1960:s the British Psychiatrist Julian Leff and his research group collected lots of data concerning risk factors in the social surroundings of schizophrenic patients after interviewing and analyzing 1000 of relatives. He concluded that the biggest risk factor without comparison was so called "High Expressed Emotion".(3)

If a person in the patients surrounding had high expressed emotion, it was only a matter of time when the patient should become psychotic and require hospitalization again.

Expressed Emotion is high if a person expresses lots of criticism or hatred, or if he/she is emotionally over involved.

Emotional overinvolvement is a more subtle way of expressing criticism. It is typical for the mother who does not dare to let her child stand on his/her own legs and by doing that tells the child that you are not clever enough to make it on him/herself.

It is all about control...

The more you try to control someone else, the worse they will feel.

This fact has been confirmed in many hundreds of scientific studies, and is not only the biggest rise factors for psychotic disorders , anxiety and depression, but also for many "normal" diseases like diabetes.

References Chapter 3

1. Helplessness: On Depression, Development, and Death. San Francisco: W.H. Freeman. ISBN 0-7167-0752-7. 1975

2. Man's Search for Meaning, Part One, "Experiences in a Concentration Camp", Viktor Frankl, Pocket Books, ISBN 978-0-671-02337-9
3. Expressed emotion research in Europe. Kuipers L Br J Clin Psychol. 1992 Nov;31(4):429-43

Illustrations:

1. https://pxhere.com/en/photo/832884

Chapter 4: Corruption

As slaves have nothing to say about their own destiny, there will be very little transparency and openness in a slave dominated, hierarchical society.

This makes an excellent breeding ground for Corruption.

There are essentially two types of corruption:

1. Corruption in the classic sense, i.e. you bribe an official in order to get a special service, instead of paying a speeding ticket.

2. Institutional Corruption. This means that the whole system is rigged and corrupt. In a moral sense there is major corruption, but no laws are broken. This is very much the case in politics, medicine and banking among others.

As we have been discussing the consequences of slavery on human health, we will now also study the effects of medical corruption on human health.

The Faust Syndrome: ‘

In order to exemplify the problem of corruption in a grand scale, we have chosen to describe one of the most corrupted systems in today's society, the western medical system:

We dare to state that a huge reason for human illness today is what we call "the Faust Syndrome". Faust (1) is the protagonist of a classic German legend, based on the historical Johann Georg Faust (c. 1480–1540).

The erudite Faust is highly successful yet dissatisfied with his life, which leads him to make a pact with the Devil, exchanging his soul for unlimited knowledge and worldly pleasures. The Faust legend has been the basis for many literary, artistic, cinematic, and musical works that have reinterpreted it through the ages. The most famous version in the arts is Johann Wolfgang von Goethes Drama "Faust", published in 1832

The Faust Syndrome can be defined as this: > 90 % of all medical doctors rather let their patients die a tormenting death, than risk their rumor among their colleagues and the medical authorities.

The remaining small percentage of medical doctors most likely have to spend a big part of their energy on lawyers and risk to have their careers, lives and rumors destroyed by the authorities and their colleagues...

Wherever you go in a hospital, you can feel the energy of fear. Fear of death, fear of suffering, fear of doing wrong, fear of being politically incorrect.

Today's doctors are according to our opinion among the most enslaved professions of today.

Everything is becoming more and more controlled, and there is almost no dignity left. They have been degraded from independent scientists and souls to bureaucrats.

We are quite confident that if we would have a medical science and profession based on reasoning, logic and scientific deduction, instead of fear and profit, the cancer problem and many other great medical enigmas would have been solved many years ago.

How come it ended up like this?

This story is a classic example of the effect of the master/slave mentality...

By the beginning of the 20th century, the richest man of the world was the oil emperor, John D. Rockefeller, who used many illegal methods to gain a monopoly over the American oil market. In May 15, 1911, the supreme court of the U.S. finds him guilty of corruption, illegal business contact and racketeering. As a result of this decision, the entire Rockefeller Standard Oil-Trust, the world's largest corporation of this time, was sentenced to be dismantled into many daughter companies like Exxon, Mobil, Chevron and others, where John D. Rockefeller still had many shares. At the same time, the chemical industry made a lot of progress, and many of the items sold by this industry were made from oil (2).

A group of men who comprised what may be called the Hopkins Circle joined in a project that altered the course of medical education in America. They erected an edifice, not of bricks and mortar, but an edifice that became the system of medical education that we know more than a century later. They made a plan for a standardized medical education, with high educational demands on the doctors and a standardized license exam, where patented chemical medicines were favored, and natural treatments like dietary regimes, osteopathy and homeopathy were disfavored. Much of the credit for this transformation has been appropriately attributed to Abraham Flexner and his critique of medical education contained in hi Flexner Report of 1910 (3). **Below is a portrait of Abraham Flexner:**

In order to disperse public and political pressure on him after the court case in 1911 Rockefeller used a trick called "philanthropy": he used the illegal gains from his oil monopoly to launch the Rockefeller Foundation.

The Rockefeller Foundation was the front organization for a new global business venture of Rockefeller and his accomplices like the steel baron Andrew Carnegie. This new venture was called the pharmaceutical investment business. Donation from the Rockefeller Foundation went only to medical schools and hospitals, which had become missionaries of patented pharmaceutical drugs, developed by a new breed of companies, manufacturers of patented, synthetic drugs.

This was also the time, when the first vitamins were discovered. It soon became clear, that these natural molecules had many health benefits and were able to prevent many chronic health conditions. These newly discovered molecules had only one disadvantage: they were non-patentable.

Thus, already in its first years of existence, the pharmaceutical investment business faced a threat: The elimination of this unwanted competition from natural micronutrients became an important issue.

In 1918, the Rockefeller Foundation uses the Spanish flu epidemic and the media they already controlled at this time, to start a witch hunt on all forms of medicine, which were not covered by their patents.

Within the next 15 years essentially all medical schools in the U.S., most hospitals and the American Medical Association all became pawns of the chess board of Rockefellers strategy to subjugate the entire health care sector under his monopoly of the pharmaceutical investment business.

Disguised as a "Mother Theresa", the Rockefeller Foundation was also used to conquer foreign countries and entire continents for the pharmaceutical investment business – just as Rockefeller had done it a few decades ago with his petrochemical investment business.

In 1925, on the other side of the Atlantic, in Germany, the first chemical / pharmaceutical cartel is founded in order to compete with the quest for control of the global drug market by the Rockefeller trust. Lead by German multinationals Bayer, BASF and Hoechst, the I.G. Farben cartel was founded with a total number of employees surpassing 80.000.(4) The race for global control was on.

In 1929, the Rockefeller cartel (U.S.A.) and the I.G. Farben cartel (Germany) decided to divide the entire globe into interest spheres, the very same crime, Rockefeller had been sentenced for 18 years earlier, when his trust had divided up the U.S. into "interest zones".

In 1932, he and I.G. Farben cartel, equally insatiable, decides no longer to be bound by the 1929 constraints. They support an uprising German politician, who promises I.G. Farben to militarily conquer the world and seize all the properties from the Jewish people for them. With millions of dollars in election campaign donations, this politician seized power in Germany, turned the German democracy into a dictatorship and kept his promise to launch his conquest war, a war that soon became known as WWII. In each and every country Hitler's Wehrmacht invaded, the first act was to rob the chemical, petrochemical and pharmaceutical industries and assign them – free of charge – to the I.G. Farben empire. Another main sponsor of the IG Farben cartel was the Swedish Wallenberg family, which nowadays dominates great parts of the world through its control of telecommunication, (Ericsson), energy (ABB), and medical industry(Astra-Zeneca).(5)

In order to cement its global leadership with patented drugs, the I.G. Farben cartel tests their patented pharmaceutical substances on concentration camp inmates in Auschwitz, Dachau and many other sites. The fees for conducting these inhumane studies were transferred directly from the bank accounts of Bayer, Hoechst and BASF to the bank accounts of the SS, who operated the concentration camps.

After Germanys capitulation, I.G. Farben's plan to take control of the global oil and drug markets had failed. The U.S. and the other allied forces won WWII. While many U.S. and allied soldiers lost their lives, their reward was little compared to the rewards of others. The corporate shares of the losers, I.G. Farben, went to the Rockefeller trust (U.S.A.) and Rothschild / J.P. Morgan (U.K.).

In the Nuremberg war crime tribunal 24 managers from Bayer, BASF, Hoechst and other executives of the I.G. Farben cartel were tried for crimes against humanity, including leading wars of aggression, slavery and mass murder. In his final pleading U.S.-Chief Prosecutor Telford Taylor summarized the crimes committed by these corporate criminals with the following words: "without I.G. Farben, the second World War would not have been possible".

Amazingly the real culprits for the death of 60 Million people in World War II – the I.G. Farben executives – received the mildest verdicts. Even those executives directly responsible for the crimes in I.G. Auschwitz received a maximum of twelve years in jail.

The medical corruption still continues.

The Danish Professor in Medicine and former chairperson of the Scandinavian part of the so-called Cochrane Collaboration (An organization dedicated to analyze medical research) has written a book about this called "Deadly Medicine and Organized Crime"(6)

Below are some more citations from Peter Goetszche's book:

"By buying most knowledgeable experts in the field, the drug industry also corrupts the peer review system. Journal editors look to experts to tell them whether a submitted research study has been done well, and experts on industry payroll may tell them it is, even when that's not the case. Many experts have shares in companies and know perfectly well what it means for the company to have a trial published in one of our most prestigious journals."

"when I showed the graph to a colleague from industry, he laughed and said that everybody knew that about 5% of trials were fraudulent, i.e. more or less made up. Data fabrication was so widespread in the drug industry that there was slang for it: 'dry labelling' or 'graphiting' in the United States and 'making' in Japan.

"The industry has armies of paid bloggers that distribute pharma material disguised as opinion on the internet, and most major media outlets have pharma ties. For example, James Murdoch, son of Rupert Murdoch, was on the board of GlaxoSmithKline and Time Inc's CEO Laura Lang formerly worked at Pfizer and Bristol-Myers Squibb. This helps explain why we so often see completely uncritical articles in the media that are copy-and-paste versions of company press releases about their wonder drugs. Like the drug industry, the media are immensely powerful, and when the two join forces, falsehoods are at their worst. The industry also tries to get access to making changes in Wikipedia to ensure pharma friendly messages appear there too."

"The drug industry also does what it can to corrupt politicians. In the United States, the drug industry contributes generously to election campaigns and there is more than one lobbyist for each member of Congress, which makes it the strongest lobby in Washington. The drug industry also contributes handsomely to political campaigns, and most of the money go to the Republicans. Between 1998 and 2006, the industry spent $ 1.2 billion on lobbying and political contributions, and in 1994, the Republicans attempted to eliminate the FDA altogether and let the drug industry regulate itself! Lobbying is also strong in Brussels"

Here are some citations regarding the famous Thalidomide catastrophe, a sleeping medication that made children become born with severe birth defects like missing limbs if their mothers had taken the medication during pregnancy:

"Private detectives kept an eye on physicians who criticized thalidomide, and when a physician had found 14 cases of extremely rare birth defects related to the drug, Grünenthal (The company that manufactured Thalidomide) threatened him with legal action and sent letters to about 70 000 German doctors declaring that thalidomide was a safe drug, although the company – in addition to the birth defects – had reports of about 2000 cases of serious and irreversible nerve damage they kept quiet about. Grünenthal harassed the alert doctor for the next 10 years. An FDA scientist that refused to approve thalidomide for the US market was also harassed and intimidated, not only by the company but also by her bosses at the FDA."

Here are some examples of threats that has happened, "when scientists have found lethal harms with marketed drugs that the companies have successfully concealed. Such threats have included frightening telephone calls from the company warning that 'very bad things could happen', cars waiting near the researcher's home through the night, a ghoulish funeral gift, or an anonymous letter containing a picture of the researcher's young daughter leaving home to go to school. Not much difference to organized gang crime there. Journalists have often been threatened with reprisals. A lawyer phoned a journalist who had written critically about the drug industry based on my research and said he called on behalf of a friend. He was interested in knowing how she had gotten access to documents that the company considered strictly confidential. He wouldn't reveal who his client was. He called again and threatened her by saying that journalists who are critical towards the drug industry may lose everything, their family, friends and job. The journalist got very scared and didn't sleep much that night."

"In 2008, one of Professor Goetze's colleagues, Jens Lundgren, received a death threat at the international AIDS congress in Mexico City in an SMS sent a few hours before he presented data showing that GlaxoSmithKline's £600 million drug, abacavir, almost doubles the risk of heart attacks. The pressures had already been immense after he published his results in the Lancet 4 months earlier, and Lundgren described how 'We were completely crushed in the GSK media machine when our study came out'. The organizers had also received threats, and as soon as Lundgren had finished his talk, he was escorted to the airport with eight bodyguards."

This rapid increase in costs for new drugs also makes them unavailable to a majority of the world population, who simply cannot afford new drugs. For example, Bristol-Myers Squibb is pricing the new cancer medicine ipilimumab at $30,000 per injection. This translates to a cost of $120,000 for a course of therapy, based on the approved dosing regimen of 3 mg/kg every 3 weeks for four doses, which is totally out of reach for most of the cancer patients in the third world.

Professor Goetze also makes this very entertaining remark by the end of his book:

"During a pre-meeting dinner, the chairman of the meeting asked me not to be too tough with the industry; I smiled and said it was too late to change my talk. I don't go to sponsored meetings, unless I have a chance of influencing the prevailing culture among doctors, which was the case here. In my talk, I took the five sponsors, Merck, Pfizer, UCB, Abbott and Roche, one by one, from the bottom up: Roche was a drug pusher that had built its fortune on selling heroin illegally in the United States; made millions of people hooked on Librium and Valium while the company denied they caused dependence; and had lured European governments into buying Tamiflu for billions of Euros, which I considered the biggest theft in European history. Abbott and its hired gun, a Danish cardiologist, blocked the access the Danish drug agency had granted us to unpublished trials of the slimming pill, sibutramine, which was later withdrawn from the market because of cardiovascular toxicity. UCB in Belgium sent us a letter stating that UCB is an ethical company and that all data are proprietary solely to the UCB who has the exclusive right to make whatever it deems desirable. I remarked that talking about being an ethical company and at the same time concealing trial data was bullshit. We performed a meta-analysis of a natural hormone, somatostatin, used for stopping bleeding although the effect is doubtful, 1 and we discovered that the biggest trial ever done had not been published. Pfizer lied at an FDA hearing about the cardiovascular harms of celecoxib; it agreed to pay a record fine of $ 2.3 billion for promotion of off-label use of four drugs; it entered a Corporate Integrity Agreement with the US Department of Health and Human Services, which probably wouldn't work, as Pfizer had entered three such agreements previously. I explained that the reason Pfizer was the world's biggest company might be that it was more criminal than other companies. Merck had caused the unnecessary deaths of tens of thousands of patients with rheumatological problems through its ruthless behavior; it selectively targeted doctors that raised critical questions about the drug; it concealed the cardiovascular risk both in publications and marketing; and the only thing that happened to its CEO, Raymond Gilmartin, was that he became immensely rich. After this introduction, I fired some more torpedoes about habitual fraud and crimes in the drug industry with devastating consequences for the patients and ended my talk by quoting the BMJ's editor, Fiona Godlee: 'Just say no.' I also told the society that if they still couldn't see there was a problem in receiving money from activities that were partly criminal, then why not get a sponsorship from Hells Angels?"

The Covid19 crisis

Everyone knows the story of the glazier, who hires people to smash windows so he can make money repairing them. Bill Gates uses the same strategy by promoting research on new viruses while funding the production of vaccines. He knows this strategy very well because he is good Windows seller.

Around 2010, a controversy arose in the research world about so-called gain-of-function research on the bird flu virus, a so-called coronavirus. This means that you deliberately manipulate a harmless virus that cannot infect humans so that it can, and thus become dangerous and a potential pandemic threat. The head of the CDC (Center for Disease Control) in the USA, Dr. Anthony Fauci played an important role in promoting this research. He argued that it was worth the risk it posed to enable research into antiviral drugs and vaccines in preparation for future pandemics.

The work entailed great risks that worried even experienced researchers. More than two hundred researchers demanded that the work be stopped, and in 2014 the National Institute of Health in the United States established a moratorium on the work, thus interrupting twenty-one ongoing scientific studies. Then instead decided Dr. Fauci and his associates circumvent this moratorium by outsourcing research to a virus laboratory in Wuhan, China, donating $ 3.7 million for this purpose.19 In 2019, Fauci donated an additional $ 3.7 million to gain-of-function research in Wuhan, bringing the total to $ 7.4 million (7).

In December 2019, several cases of an unusual type of pneumonia were seen in Wuhan, China. It was relatively soon found that the victims were carrying a new type of coronavirus that came to be known as SARS COVID 2. At first it was thought that the victims had been infected at a so-called "wetmarket" in Wuhan, where live animals are sold. The virus was believed to come from infected bats.

Later, it has been more and more concluded that the virus probably originated from the virus laboratory in Wuhan, where they conducted research on coronavirus. There are many indications that it has been manipulated by humans and it contains several types of gene sequences that can hardly have arisen naturally. Several world-famous virus researchers have stated this, including the Nobel laureate and one of the discoverers of the AIDS virus, Luc Montagnier(8) and the world-famous virus researcher Judy Mikovits, author of the books Plague and Plague of Corruption(9).

There are divided opinions as to whether the virus escaped from the laboratory in Wuhan due to an accident or whether it was a deliberate act.

At the end of October 2020, the WHO states that approximately 40 million people had been infected with the virus and that over one million people have died. The worst affected countries were the United States, Spain, the United Kingdom, France and Italy, with tens of thousands of deaths. This led to panic all over the world, which in turn led to more or less closure of entire countries, with catastrophic consequences for the economy. The health authorities in most countries in the always pointed out that there was no cure for the disease and that the only thing we can do to protect ourselves is to keep distance from others, isolate ourselves at home, wash our hands while waiting for the authorities and the pharmaceutical industry to develop a vaccine.

The SARS COVID 2 virus has many similarities with the previous SARS COVID 1 virus, which ravaged 2003-2004, with a higher mortality rate of about ten percent but with a lower tendency to spread infection than SARS Covid 2. Even then, it was found that the malaria drugs hydroxychloroquine and chloroquine could have an inhibitory effect on the virus. Hydroxychloroquine is also used in the treatment of rheumatic diseases and chronic tick-related infections, for example against the intracellular, malaria-like parasite Bebesia, which can cause malaria-like symptoms with fever episodes and air-hunger/panic attacks. At the outbreak of the Covid19 epidemic in China, it was also noted that almost no rheumatological patients treated with chloroquine or hydroxychloroquine had been affected by Covid19.

In China, the use of hydroxychloroquine on a large scale began and the medicine was soon included in the official Chinese therapy recommendations. Traditional herbal medicines, hydrogen inhalation and intravenous vitamin C treatment were also used in high doses(10). The affected provinces were also closed down and used of advanced monitoring systems with face recognition and mobile phone applications to perform infection tracking and provide individually tailored infection control advice to all Chinese residents. The death toll dropped sharply, In April 2020, the affected provinces were reopened. By May 2020, China had recorded only about 4,600 deaths per 1.4 billion inhabitants, which can be compared with the figure in the United States, where 97,000 deaths were recorded at the same time.

However, there are major uncertainties surrounding these figures and there are reports of over-reporting of COVID19 deaths in the US and under-reporting in China. In the USA, for example, you can have your hospital bill paid for by the state if you yourself do not have health insurance if you state Covid19 as the cause of illness and death. There are also reports that they want to exaggerate the effects of the Covid19 catastrophe to prevent Donald Trump from being re-elected in the 2020 presidential election. China wants to keep its numbers down due to propaganda benefits.

A doctor in New York, Dr. Vladimir Zelenko (11), reported in March 2020 that he had successfully treated hundreds of Covid19 patients with a combination of hydroxychloroquine, the antibiotic Azithromycin and zinc. He believed that he had managed to reduce the expected mortality by ninety percent with the help of this treatment. Infection professor Didier Rault in Marseille, France, did a similar treatment, treating on over two thousand patients with similar results (12).

This was noticed by a number of governments and heads of government around the world, including by President Donald Trump who said he had a good feeling about this medicine. A few weeks later, he announced that he himself had started taking it for preventive purposes, which went like a shock wave through the world press. Other governments that decided to use the medicine were Russia, Israel, Australia and India. In India, it was also decided to give it as preventive medicine to all relatives of covid19 patients as well as to police and healthcare staff. It was also noted that there were almost no covid19 infections in countries where malaria prophylaxis is routinely taken, and sun is omnipresent, such as Congo, Ethiopia, Madagascar and Nigeria (13).

The President of Madagascar, Andry Rajoelina, also campaigned for a local health drink containing summer wormwood, or Artemesia Annua, which is also a well-known antimalarial drug. He believed that this drink was a miracle cure for Covid19 and he wanted to make it available to all his citizens. That he may not be completely wrong is confirmed by the extremely low death toll for Madagascar with only two deaths of 27,000 inhabitants at the end of May 2020. In Russia, successful attempts have also been made with another malaria medicine called Mefloquin. At the same time, Russia had only about 3,300 deaths per 145 million inhabitants, and the second largest number of confirmed infections in the world after the United States, with 336,000 confirmed cases, according to the WHO/John Hopkins Institute statistics.

What do you do then in many western countries like Sweden and the US? Prohibits the prescribing of chloroquine and hydroxychloroquine to all but specialists in rheumatology and physicians participating in clinical trials in hospitals. This means that as a sick patient you can only receive this potentially life-saving medicine when it may already be too late, having already getting such severe symptoms that you have to go to a hospital, as hydroxychloroquine is only effective at the first stage of the disease, before getting too severe symptoms, just like when you treat Herpes Zoster with Aciklovir, or Influenza with Tamiflu. At the same time, a propaganda campaign was launched in the mass media around the world to show how "dangerous" hydroxychloroquine was. The reason was that it can affect the so-called QT interval, or the time it takes for an electrical impulse from the atrium of the heart to reach the heart chamber. If this interval is prolonged too much, life-threatening heart arrhythmias can occur. However, this is a very rare side effect that only occurs in about one case per 100,000 patients if you make sure to exclude patients with long QT intervals, through a so-called ECG, and other risk groups before starting treatment.

In a review article on 35,448 patients who received treatment with high doses of chloroquine for malaria no serious cardiac side effects were noted at all. (14)

Yet, for example, infection professor Ander Sönnerborg at Karolinska Institutet states that hydroxychloroquine is life-threatening and that Trump may die because he uses it. (15)

When they googled hydroxychloroquine and Covid19 in May 2020, they found hundreds of articles in all the major mainstream media that describe the medicine as life-threatening, such as "snake oil" and so on. Furthermore, studies have been carried out in which hydroxychloroquine has been given to very seriously ill patients far too late in the course and after that compared with less ill patients, and subsequently it has been claimed that "it increases mortality".

A large non-randomized registry study published in the Lancet on May 22, 2020 (16), stated that mortality was higher among patients who received hydroxychloroquine and chloroquine compared with those who did not receive any treatment. and that the treatment also led to an increased incident of life-threatening arrhythmias. This study went extremely against the observations described above and aroused a strong suspicion regarding the authenticity of the study. T results of this study suited the pharmaceutical industry too well to be true. Several independent researchers also criticized the study in an open letter (17). This criticism was later confirmed by the journal Lancet, which later withdrew the article. It turned out that it was a small company with six employees who had produced the article, one of whom was a adult model and another a science fiction writer. Together, they were able to write a science fiction article that made the pharmaceutical industry and our authorities dream wet dreams of avoiding the likely public execution that would result if hydroxychloroquine were to proven to effective. This must be one of the biggest scams in medical history, but despite that, it was barely mentioned in our mainstream media.

It is also interesting to note how the press and the establishment have systematically ridiculed all information that one could partially protect oneself by taking high doses of, for example, vitamin C, vitamin D and zinc, despite the fact that there is plenty of scientific evidence for that these supplements can have a positive effect on one's ability to cope with viral infections. Many have, for example, related the seasonal variations of influenza diseases to, among other things, a lack of sunlight and vitamin D, as well as less intake of vitamin C from fruits and vegetables during the winter. This is also confirmed in an article in the Swedish medical journal "Läkartidningen".(18) These facts were also later even more confirmed in a large number of clinical studies, all of which show a 50-95% reduction in mortality for those with normal vitamin D values.

It is quite clear to us that every effort is being made to slander all possible natural, relatively side-effect-free and inexpensive alternatives in the treatment of Covid19 to ensure the largest possible market for future vaccine sales and sales of expensive antiviral drugs. Likewise, there is nothing in our mainstream media about the successful attempts to treat Covid19 with ozone treatment in Spain and Italy, as well as with vitamin C infusion in China and the USA, and with hydrogen inhalation in China. (10)

When I informed about these results in a series of very popular YouTube videos, several of them were removed by YouTube, and the Swedish Health and Care Inspectorate (IVO) threatened to try to rescind my medical because of my statements, that it is likely, the Corona crisis can be solved by combining these harmless and inexpensive treatment methods. China did this, and thereby solved their crisis, but these facts are well hidden behind the curtain of semi-official censorship from the mainstream media.

Should it not be the case that if there are cheap and harmless treatment methods that works, according to international experience, that it would be the duty of every doctor to use these rather than passively watching when patients die a painful death because the doctor follows have to follow the guidelines of the authorities?

Below is information obtained through personal communication with those involved, including the Swedish doctor Jon Tallinger, the immunology professor Dolores Cahill from Ireland and others, who have all testified about how the authorities used the Covid19 crisis in order to prematurely kill many of our elderly.

While the authorities have incorrectly warned about the risks of hydroxychloroquine, according to a number of testimonies and reports from the whistleblower doctor Jon Tallinger, they have also contributed to mass murder of our elderly population by putting them on so-called "palliative treatment" in nursing homes instead of giving them hospital care. This has meant that instead of giving them oxygen, vitamin D, hydroxychloroquine and more, they have been given sedatives and painkillers such as midazolam and morphine, which impair the respiratory function of these patients, who already have difficulty breathing, which leads to death.

These decisions have often been made by telephone by a doctor who has never seen the patient. At the same time, the relatives are also isolated from their relative, so they cannot follow the process.

In an interview with the World Doctors Alliance in Berlin on October 10, 2020, which was shown over a million times on Twitter before it was removed, I talked about this, and said at the same time that it should now be considered criminal to pay taxes in Sweden, because it can be described as aiding and abetting to murder. I don't want to support authorities who deliberately and behind the back kill their citizens with a faked smile on their face.

During the latter part of 2020, it has also emerged that many of the deaths classified by the authorities as covid19 deaths were not caused by Covid19, but were patients who had died of Alzheimer's disease, heart attack or cancer at the same time as they have had a positive Covid19 test.

Irish molecular biology and immunology professor Dolores Cahill pressured forensic scientists, threatening to sue them due to fraud, to investigate how many in Ireland had actually died of Covid19, compared to the official number. Then the number dropped from about 1700 cases to 96!

Furthermore, she and a large number of other top-level specialists from around the world say that they have not yet succeeded in isolating the Covid19 virus, and without having done so, it is impossible to produce correct Covid19 tests. In fact, the current tests used by millions worldwide are not approved for clinical use and give rise to a large number of false positive results, which can be verified by all the millions of people who have received positive test results even though they feel healthy. Tanzania's President John Magufuli, who is also a chemist, succeeded in producing positive Covid-19 test results from a papaya and a goat, among other things. My friends in the newly formed World Doctors Alliance who were involved in organizing the mass meetings in London and Berlin, where I had the great honor of giving speeches in front of tens of thousands of spectators, have also sent in unprocessed tests, i.e. cotton swabs that have never been exposed to anyone nasal mucosa, and regained positive Covid19 results.

Against this background and with the support of thousands of doctors and several virology professors at the highest level, the German / American top lawyer Reiner Fuellmich, who led the famous lawsuit against Volkswagen's exhaust fraud and Deutsche Bank, has started a joint class-action lawsuit with several other top lawyers against the US, Canadian and European authorities. He does not hesitate to call the corona fraud a "crime against humanity". This means that millions of victims of crime can take part in this joint trial with the intention of compensating the victims for the damage they and their companies have suffered due to the authorities' fraud and socially harmful and unnecessary lockdown measures.

I am cooperating with all of these people, and we have together started the two organizations, World Doctors Alliance and World Freedom alliance, where I am one of the core founders. My daughter, Maneka Helleberg is currently the one who for the most part keeps the threads for the last mentioned two projects and I am a very proud father.

Propaganda and Censorship:

If you are corrupt, one of your key interests will be to keep the corruption hidden from insight. That leads to censorship and propaganda.

Maybe you have already heard this joke: "President Kennedy of USA and Nikita Chrustiev of the former Soviet Union had a meeting in which they challenged each other who was the fastest 100-meter runner. As president Kennedy was much younger and fitter, he did win with a big margin.

Next day, the official Moscow newspaper Pravda wrote: "The leader of our great nation, Nikita Chrustiev and the president of the United States of America took part in a competition on 100 meters yesterday. Our leader had a very impressive second place in the race, while President Kennedy was second last."

It is a well-known fact that every dictator has had a propaganda department. Hitler had his Goebbels, Stalin his "Pravda", as well as Saddam Hussein and Mao Tse-tung had their propaganda agencies. People who dared to speak out against the dictators often risked harsh treatment and torture in jails, and even death.

In the West, many people believe that we have a free press and that what we are served in the evening news and in our daily newspapers is trustworthy information. Nothing is more far from the truth.

We also have our propaganda agencies, although our propagandists are much more skillful than Joseph Goebbels & Co.

The trend of media conglomeration has been steady. In 1983, 50 corporations controlled most of the American media, including magazines, books, music, news feeds, newspapers, movies, radio and television. By 1992 that number had dropped by half. By 2000, six corporations had ownership of most media, and today five dominate the industry: Time Warner, Disney, Murdoch's News Corporation, Bertelsmann of Germany and Viacom. With markets branching rapidly into international territories, these few companies are increasingly responsible for deciding what information is shared around the world (19).

There are also major news organizations not owned by the "big five." The New York Times is owned by the publicly-held New York Times Corporation, The Washington Post is owned by the publicly-held Washington Post Company and The Chicago Tribune and Los Angeles Times are both owned by the Tribune Company. Hearst Publications owns 12 newspapers including the San Francisco Chronicle, as well as magazines, television stations and cable and interactive media.

But even those publications are subject to the conglomerate machine, and many see the "corporatizing" of media as an alarming trend. Ben Bagdikian, Pulitzer-prize winning journalist, former Dean of the Graduate School of Journalism at UC Berkeley and author of The New Media Monopoly, describes the five media giants as a "cartel" that wields enough influence to change U.S. politics and define social values.

Internet Ownership:

Originally, the Internet was the champion of free thinkers, embraced as a liberating force from corporate owned media. But over time even online news sites joined radio, television, newspapers and magazines as properties of the small handful of media conglomerates.

In raw numbers, 80 percent of the top 20 online news sites are owned by the 100 largest media companies. Time Warner owns two of the most visited sites: CNN.com and AOL News, while Gannett, which is the twelfth largest media company, owns USA Today.com along with many local online newspapers. Behind the screen, a very large part of the hardware infrastructure is controlled by the Swedish Internet giant Ericsson.

What we should be most concerned about, Bagdikian says, is the narrowing of choices, because that removes from voters the full spectrum of views and information with which to choose its government—a dangerous trend that threatens democracy itself.

Political Corruption:

"In the US, your first obligation as a politician is to satisfy your campaign funders, secondly your party, and thirdly, the voters. Without support from the rich families in New York, your career is over in fifteen minutes." Former Senator and President Candidate Mike Gravel, USA.

In their article " Testing Theories of American Politics, Professor Martin Gilens from Princeton University and Professor and Benjamin I. Page from Northwestern University (20) concludes that:
"Each of four theoretical traditions in the study of American politics—which can be characterized as theories of Majoritarian Electoral Democracy, Economic-Elite Domination, and two types of interest-group pluralism, Majoritarian Pluralism and Biased Pluralism—offers different predictions about which sets of actors have how much influence over public policy: average citizens; economic elites; and organized interest groups, mass-based or business-oriented. A great deal of empirical research speaks to the policy influence of one or another set of actors, but until recently it has not been possible to test these contrasting theoretical predictions against each other within a single statistical model. We report on an effort to do so, using a unique data set that includes measures of the key variables for 1,779 policy issues. Multivariate analysis indicates that economic elites and organized groups representing business interests have substantial independent impacts on U.S. government policy, while average citizens and mass-based interest groups have little or no independent influence. The results provide substantial support for theories of Economic-Elite Domination and for theories of Biased Pluralism, but not for theories of Majoritarian Electoral Democracy or Majoritarian Pluralism."

It is also a well-known fact that many politicians get their reward for "good work" by getting lucrative contracts from private companies after that their career is finished, i.e. the former prime minister of Sweden, Göran Persson who after his political career became the chairperson of one major banks in Scandinavia, Nordea, without any experience of the banking business from before.

Unequal Distribution of Resources - Conquering the World:

Society today is based upon rivalry, not cooperation, why is that a problem? Since the introduction of the conquering cultures, the aim of every dictator has been to conquer as much as possible. In the end, the ultimate goal was to conquer the entire world. Alexander the Great tried, The Roman Emperors tried, The Mongols tried, The British tried, The Communists in Soviet tried it, and now the financial oligarchy in the US and Western Europe are on the verge of succeeding, although they still have some opposition to face.

After the first and second world wars and the invention of the Atomic Bomb, acquiring world dominance with military means became too risky, as it literally threatened to destroy our entire planet. The risks and costs of the destruction outnumbered the gains. That was the starting point for another strategy of world dictatorship through the use of banking in co-operation with media, corrupted state institutions, and limited use of military resources.

In his book, "Confessions of an Economic Hit Man" (21), the Author and former NSA employee John Perkins describe his career with engineering consulting firm Chas. T. Main in Boston. According to Perkins, his job at Main was to convince leaders of underdeveloped countries to accept substantial development loans for large construction and engineering projects that would primarily help the richest families and local elites, rather than the poor, while making sure that these projects were contracted to U.S. companies. Later these loans would give the U.S. political influence and access to natural resources for U.S. companies. He characterizes his role as being an "economic hit man".

According to him "Economic hit men (EHMs) are highly paid professionals who cheat countries around the globe out of trillions of dollars. They funnel money from the World Bank, the U.S. Agency for International Development (USAID), and other foreign "aid" organizations into the coffers of huge corporations and the pockets of a few wealthy families who control the planet's natural resources. Their tools included fraudulent financial reports, rigged elections, payoffs, extortion, sex, and murder. They play a game as old as empire, but one that has taken on new and terrifying dimensions during this time of globalization."

He says: "I was initially recruited while I was in business school back in the late sixties by the National Security Agency, the nation's largest and least understood spy organization; but ultimately I worked for private corporations. The first real economic hit man was back in the early 1950s, Kermit Roosevelt, Jr., the grandson of Teddy, who overthrew the government of Iran, a democratically elected government, Mossadegh's government who was Time's magazine person of the year; and he was so successful at doing this without any bloodshed—well, there was a little bloodshed, but no military intervention, just spending millions of dollars and replaced Mossadegh with the obedient Shah of Iran. At that point, we understood that this idea of economic hit man was an extremely good one. We didn't have to worry about the threat of war with Russia when we did it this way. The problem with that was that Kermit Roosevelt was a C.I.A. agent. He was a government employee. Had he been caught; he would have been in a lot of trouble. It would have been very embarrassing. So, at that point, the decision was made to use organizations like the C.I.A. and the

N.S.A. to recruit potential economic hit men like me and then send us to work for private consulting companies, engineering firms, construction companies, so that if we were caught, there would be no connection with the government."

<u>According to Perkins, the US/World Bank strategy for world domination used three different steps:</u>

1. Take control of a country by offering loans that can never be paid back, so that the country literally will end up in the pockets of the big banks, that in turn are controlled by the Super rich that also control most western countries.

2. If the leaders of the country refuse this offer, they will be ridiculed and scandalized in the international press, and most likely die in an arranged plane crash or other "accident". The leaders know this. Their choice is to sell out their country and become stinking rich, or die as defamed and unwanted persons.

3. If this strategy does not work, the US will send in the Marines.

This strategy has been applied in most countries in South America and many countries in Africa, Europe and Asia.

In his book "Superclass: The Global Power Elite and the World They Are Making (22) David Rothkopf claims that the world population of 6 billion people is subject to the immense influence of an elite (i.e. The Superclass) of six thousand individuals.

Until the late 20th century, governments of the great powers provided most of the superclass, accompanied by a few heads of international movements (i.e., the Pope of the Roman Catholic Church) and entrepreneurs (Rothschilds, Rockefellers). According to Rothkopf, in the early 21st century, economic clout—fueled by the explosive expansion of international trade, travel and communication—rules. Further, the nation-state's power has diminished shrinking politicians to minority power broker status. Leaders in international business, finance and the defense industry not only dominate the superclass, they move freely into high positions in their nations' governments and back to private life largely beyond the notice of elected legislatures (including the U.S. Congress), which remain abysmally ignorant of affairs beyond their borders.

Among those 6000 people, there are maybe a handful that have the real power in their hands, and there are concerns that these people with the help of global surveillance networks like the NSA, Google, Facebook and YouTube, and control over new military weapons like police robots and drones have the agenda to finally fulfill the ancient dream of world dictatorship, with a global secret police, global surveillance, propaganda and fake news. In order to change this depressive scenario, we must first understand the mechanisms that sustain it.

"False Flag" operations and infiltration the opposition.

More than a hundred years ago, some rich men, who already owned almost the entire world, sat thinking about how to consolidate their power and defend themselves against the ultimate nightmare, the socialist revolution that was lurking around the corner, after writers such as Karl Marx, Mikhail Bakunin, Piotr Kropotkin, and Pierre Joseph Proudhon had incited the masses. What do you do? Starts the world's largest "false flag" operation: a pseudo-socialist revolution, that is, the Russian Revolution. (23)
By supporting a gang of bandits financially and logistically, with Lenin, Trotsky and Stalin as leaders, two things were achieved:

1. One could plunder the Russian elite and the middle class on its riches. The bankers who supported the revolution got their money back many times over in the form of stolen property from those executed or imprisoned by the Bolshevik terrorist regime.

2. A nightmare version of socialism was created, which justified the persecution of the organized left in the West.

I hardly do not believe that a more effective method of stopping true, liberating socialism than this could ever be invented.

My grandfather, Knut Stenborg, whom I never met in this life, describes very eloquently how it happened, 1917-1918 in Russia, in his two books "In the center of the storm" and "In the footsteps of the storm". (24) A new edition of these books is planned. Unbelievable interesting reading. It took many years before this token fell down with me. Has it done that with you?

In fact, I had never heard of this theory before ... It is also interesting to note that my grandfather describes how the Bolsheviks were most zealous in killing the freedom loving socialists, who had gained a majority in Russia's first free election in 1918. This was much more important. than to take revenge on the tsar's henchmen ...

The only thing that can stop a world government is a world government

Many believe that the Covid-19 crisis and the expansion of 5G are some of the last steps in the development of a totalitarian world state where everyone is forced to carry an implanted microchip. Bill Gates publicly supports such plans, which include the person's vaccination status. If a person is not sufficiently vaccinated, for example, he or she may not travel abroad or visit restaurants and sporting events. This also means that you can follow the movements of all people exactly. The official explanation is to facilitate infection tracing.

We are also, according to, for example, one of the development managers at Google, the author Ray Kurzweil, on the way to a development where we can make a direct connection between our brains and the Internet and a connection with artificial intelligence. This could, for example, be used for absolutely incredible control mechanisms by a totalitarian world state. For example, we could be punished with an electric shock as soon as we think a rebellious thought, and if we cannot get control of our thoughts, we are liquidated ...

As mentioned earlier, we have a huge concentration of capital and political power in the world so that a very small power elite controls both the Internet, the largest companies, Mainstream Media and our politicians. No country is so large that it can control this elite on its own.

The only thing that could do that is a democratic world government, where the people of the earth come together in order to stop these totalitarian forces!

Of course, the psychopathic bankers understood this and did exactly what they had already done with socialism. They took over and infiltrated the idealistic idea of a world government so that they could control the agenda themselves. The Rockefeller family donated, for example, the land in New York on which the UN skyscraper was built, and Bill Gates is the largest contributor to the World Health Organization (WHO).

I was once invited to Washington DC by Benjamin Barber, then an adviser to Bill Clinton, Obama and Hillary Clinton, for something called "the democracy collaborative", probably funded by George Soros. Benjamin Barber's e-mail address ended in sorosny, which I later understood to mean Soros New York.

The conference was about how we could improve world democracy and I put forward the following proposals: "A wide range of our major challenges such as the issue of war and peace, environmental degradation, fair international trade and more cannot be resolved at national level, but require some form of democratically controlled world democracy. " That I previously talked about this in Sweden, and also developed the world's first software for liquid democracy, or demosocracy was probably the reason why I was invited with travel and hotel paid, as well as a generous compensation.

The other guests were the part of those who ruled the world behind the scenes and who were dominated by the Democratic Party in the United States. These included the Rockefeller Foundation, the Ford Foundation and the closest advisers to the likes of Nelson Mandela, Bill Clinton, Vaclav Havel, Lech Walesa and Michael Gorbachev.

On the meeting I said, "that since there is currently no world government, there is nothing that can stop us from organizing and achieving just that. The whole thing is like an unexplored continent, it's just to move in, clearing things up and starting to cultivate the land. When I then started talking about liquid democracy, the interest of my audience probably diminished considerably except for Mikhail Gorbachev's right-hand advisor, Andrei Grachev, who was there. He ended the meeting by saying that he thought we shall make the new world policies in accordance with my ideas. I later found out in a personal conversation with him that he had sympathies with anarchism in his heart and, for example, held Michael Bakunin very high, just like for example the famous writer and philologist, Noam Chomsky.

I also met the future adviser to President Obama, Beth Noveck, on this occasion. When I later read her book on "Wiki Democracy" (26), I saw that she had mentioned me and liquid democracy in one of her chapters. After reading the book, I also understood why she was the adviser to Obama and not me.

To get far as a democratic adviser, it is important to be smart and have ideas that can make democracy look better. However, one must not be so naive as to think that it is a matter of genuine democracy. Everything that Rockefeller and Rothschild and others cannot control will disappear from the agenda!

I was later also invited by Mikhail Gorbachev, with first-class flights and luxury hotels, to the World Political Forum in Turin in 2003. Fifty presidents and ex-presidents, Catholic cardinals and other influential people, and little me was there. As such, I am not that small, neither then nor now, I am 199 cm tall and weigh 115 kg.

I handed out my little book, "Democracy 2.0, How to Make a Bunch of Lazy and Selfish People Work Together, A Handbook About How to Maximize Collective Intelligence in Politics". (27)

In it, I present how we, the people on earth, could concretely take over the whole world with the help of liquid democracy and also compete with the big companies with the help of new cooperative forms of cooperation based on democracy, which will be described later in this book.

Now I had gone too far. After this, I received no more invitations to any meetings of this caliber. I was persecuted in the media, got a fake tax debt and had my whole life and reputation ruined.

As I said, we can play a little with so-called free elections and Internet democracy, as long as we can guarantee that it is not us but Rockefeller and Wallenberg who decides,

In order to be able to change this depressive scenario, we must first understand the mechanisms that holds it up.

References chapter 4:

1. https://en.wikipedia.org/wiki/Faust

2. https://en.wikipedia.org/wiki/John_D._Rockefeller

3. Yale J Biol Med. 2011 Sep;84(3):269-76. The Flexner Report--100 years later. Duffy TP1.

4. http://www4.dr-rath-foundation.org/open_letters/pharma_laws_history.html

5. https://carlnorberg.se/2020/09/14/ig-farben-anstiftan-till-varldskrig/

6. Deadly Medicines and Organized Crime: How Big Pharma Has Corrupted Healthcare - Peter Gotzsche ISBN-10: 1846198844 Radcliffe Publishing, New York

7. HTTPS://WWW.NEWSWEEK. COM/DR-FAUCI-BACKED-CONTROVERSIAL-WUHAN-LAB-MIL- LIONS-US-DOLLARS-RISKY-CORONAVIRUS-RESEARCH-1500741

8. Miller, Robert. *The Coronavirus Is Man Made According to Luc Montagnier the Man Who Discovered HIV.* https://www.gilmorehealth.com/chinese-coronavirus- is-a-man-made-virus-according-to-luc-montagnier-the-man-who-discovered-hiv/

9. Mikovits, Judy; Heckenlively, Kent. *Plague of Corruption Restoring Faith in the Promise of Science* By Judy Mikovits and Kent Heckenlively Foreword by Robert Jr. F. Kennedy Publisher: Skyhorse (April 14, 2020) ISBN13: 22.

10. Srinivasan,Balaji. S. *The Official Chinese Government Guide to Diagnosing and Treating the Novel Coronavirus.* https://medium.com/@balajis/the-offici-al-chinese-government-guide-to-diagnosing-and-treating-the-novel-coronavi- rus-9d06868f8df4

11. *Dr. Zelenko Discusses COVID-19 Outpatient Management* https://www.youtu- be.com/watch?v=MhLD1P5nH30 [Hämtad 2020-09-12]

12. Rault, Didier, *Abstract – Early Treatment Covid 19.* https://www.mediterranee-infection.com/wp-content/uploads/2020/04 /Abstract_Raoult_EarlyTrt- Covid19_09042020_vD1v.pdf

13. Fox News. *Do countries with high rates of malaria have fever coronavirus deaths?* https://www.foxnews.com/world/do-countries-with-high-rates-of-malaria-ha- ve-fewer-coronavirus-deaths?fbclid=IwAR2N-PaXdVULLWy5q96QFaU4Ov- 8Qf1hkE1ubZGe-rPwi_ve4kKKrwS0bhig

14. Ilsa L. Haeusler; Xin Hui S. Chan; Philippe J. Guérin; Nicholas J. White. *The arrhythmogenic cardiotoxicity of the quinoline and structurally related antimalarial drugs: a systematic review* BMC Medicine, volume 16, Article number: 200 (2018) https://bmcmedicine.biomedcentral.com/articles/10.1186/s12916-018-1188-2

15. Expressen. *Experten: Trump kan dö av malariamedicinen hydroxiklorokin.* htt- ps://www.expressen.se/tv/nyheter/coronaviruset/trump-kan-do-av-malariamedicinen-hydroxiklorokin

16. Mandeep R Mehra; Sapan S Desai; Frank Ruschitzka; Amit N Patel. *Hydroxychloroquine or chloroquine with or without a macrolide for treatment of COVID-19: a multinational registry analysis. The Lancet May 22, 2020 https://doi.org/10.1016/ S0140-6736(20)31180-6* https://www.thelancet.com/journals/lancet/article/ PIIS0140-6736(20)31180-6/8 fulltext

17. Zenodo. Wattson, James, on the behalf of 146 signatories. *An open letter to Mehra et al and The Lancet.* "Hydroxychloroquine or chloroquine with or without a macrolide for treatment of COVID-19: a multinational registry analysis". Lancet. 2020 May 22:S0140-6736(20)31180-6. doi: 10.1016/S0140-6736(20)31180-6. PMID: 32450107. https://zenodo.org/record/3864691?fbclid=IwAR0P1428X-GzfYzxUMMmWF1zjEfLA-Os9Jkh88U8DTXGmJceBUGaZaulrIa4#.X1y-bzC0zKqT

18. Läkartidningen. Mats B Humble, Henrik Pelling, Susanne Bejerot. (2020-05-07) *D-vitamin kan skydda mot svår infektion vid covid-19.* https://lakartidningen.

se/opinion/debatt/2020/05/d-vitamin-kan-skydda-mot-svar-infektion-vid-covid-19/

19. Independent Lens. Democracy on deadline. *Who owns the media?* https://www.pbs.org/independentlens/democracyondeadline/mediaownership.html [Hämtad 2020-09-12]

20. Gilens, Martin; I Page, Benjamin. *Testing Theories of American Politics: Elites, Interest Groups, and Average Citizens. Perspectives on Politics* .September 2014 Vol. 12/No. 3
https://scholar.princeton.edu/sites/default/files/mgilens/files/gilens_and_page_2014_-testing_theories_of_american_politics.doc.pdf

21. Perkins, John (2005). *Confessions of an Economic Hit Man*. Ebury Press. ISBN 9780091909109.26. ISBN: 9781785033858

21. Rothkopf, David (2008) *Superclass: The Global Power Elite and the World They Are Making.* Farrar, Straus and Giroux. ISBN-10: 9780374531614.

22. Lina, Jüri (2013). Under skorpionens tecken: Sovjetmaktens uppkomst och fall. 3., utök. uppl. Stockholm: Referent

25. Stenborg, Knut. *I stormens Centrum*. Förlagsaktiebolaget Västra Sverige (1936) 39. Sheldrake, Rupert (2015) *The Science Delusion*
https://www.pdfdrive.com/ the-science-delusion-e19343462.html

26: Noveck, Beth Simone "Wiki Government". *Brookings.* November 2, 2010 ISBN: 9780815705109

27: Nordfors, Mikael; *"Democracy 2,0, How to Make a Bunch of Lazy and Selfish People Work Together, A Handbook About How to Maximize Collective Intelligence in Politics."*
https://www.medicdebate.org/files/Democracy%2031_1.pdf

Illustrations:

1. https://commons.wikimedia.org/wiki/File:Zombie_Fest_2009_Retard_d octor_zombie_(4002688975).jpg
2. https://en.wikipedia.org/wiki/Abraham_Flexner
3. https://www.flickr.com/photos/donkeyhotey/8362040192/
4. https://en.wikipedia.org/wiki/The_Great_Dictator#/media/File:Dictator _charlie5.jpg

The big issue for the ruling class, or the masters have always been how to keep their slaves under control. The most popular method has been to use the carrot and the whip. Animals get rewarded with a piece of food when doing what their masters want them to do, and punished when they don't. The same is true about almost every human being. After a while, many of us will lose contact with our true inner self and our authentic needs in order to play the game of getting bigger and bigger rewards, at the same time as we try to avoid getting punished. We mean that this is the core feature in the gigantic epidemic of greed and or corruption that is currently crippling our society.

An old Indian tale (1) relates to this phenomenon: "A beggar came to an emperor's palace. The emperor was just in the garden so he heard the beggar. The man on the gate was going to give something, but the beggar said, "I have one condition. I always take from the master, never from servants."

The emperor heard. He was taking a walk so he came to look at this beggar, because beggars don't have conditions. If you are a beggar, how can you have conditions? "Seems to be a rare beggar." So he came to look – and he WAS a rare beggar. The emperor had never seen such an emperor-like man before; he was nothing. This man had some glory around him, a grace. Tattered his dress was, almost naked, but the begging bowl was very very precious.

The emperor said, "Why this condition?"

The beggar said, "Because servants are themselves beggars and I don't want to be rude to anybody. Only masters can give. How can servants give? So, if you are ready, you can give and I will accept it. But then too I have a condition, and that is: my begging bowl has to be completely filled."

A small begging bowl! The emperor started laughing. He said," You seem to be mad. Do you think I cannot fill your begging bowl?" And then he ordered his ministers to bring precious stones, incomparable, unique, and fill the begging bowl with them. But they got into a difficulty, because the more they filled the begging bowl, the stones would fall in it and they would not even make a sound, they would simply disappear. And the begging bowl remained empty.

Then the emperor was in a fix, his whole ego was at stake. He, a great emperor who ruled the whole earth, could not fill a begging bowl! He ordered<," Bring everything, but this begging bowl has to be filled!"

His treasures... for days together all his treasuries were emptied, but the begging bowl remained empty. There was no more left. The emperor had become a beggar, all was lost. The emperor fell to the beggar's feet and said, "Now I am also a beggar and I beg only one thing. Tell me the secret of this bowl, it seems to be magical!"

The beggar said, "Nothing. It is made of human mind, nothing magical."

Every human mind is just this begging bowl. You go on filling it, it remains empty. You throw the whole world, worlds together, and they simply disappear without making any sound. You go on giving and it is always begging.

Give love, and the begging bowl is there, your love has disappeared. Give your whole life, and the begging bowl is there, looking at you with complaining eyes. "You have not given anything. I am still empty." And the only proof that you have given is if the begging bowl is full – and it is never full. Of course, the logic is clear: you have not given.

You have achieved many many things – they have all disappeared in the begging bowl. The mind is a self-destructive process. Before the mind disappears, you will remain a beggar. Whatsoever you can gain will be in vain; you will remain empty.

And if you dissolve this mind, through emptiness you become filled for the first time. You are no more, but you have become the whole. If you are, you will remain a beggar. If you are not, you become the emperor."

We dare to state that the real reason for this insatiable greed is that we once have bereaved, our authentic feelings and our natural connection to the universe, and tries to compensate with greed and ambition.

You cannot replace an authentic need for being accepted end respected for what you truly are with a fabricated need glory, money and honor, just as you cannot eat instead of having sex, you will get very fat and probably having less chance of getting sex because of that. There is a point where you do not get happier by material welfare but you need human connection. In a study published in Nature 2018, Andrew Jebb with coworkers (2) concluded that Higher incomes than §100 000 year does not make you happier! By investigating 1.7 million individuals worldwide were investigated between the relationship how happy they felt and their annual income.

a

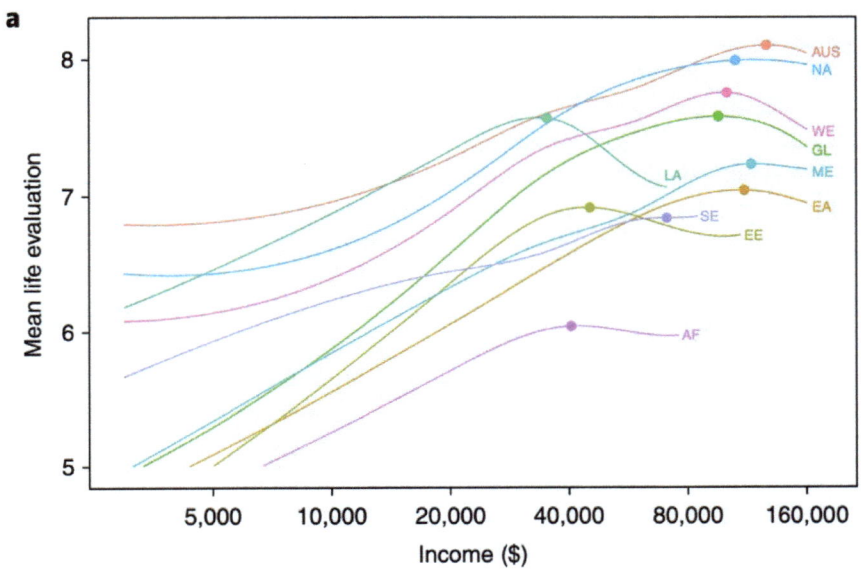

No one was ever asked if they were happy or how happy they are. But instead were asked questions, in the first place, about their overall feeling about their lives in a generic way, and in the second place, about the kind of emotions they had predominately experienced the previous day. The former measure is effective because it avoids disparities in how people classify or define the word "happiness" or "happy." And the latter measure is effective because random factors (like, say, having just lost a loved one the week before) get randomized in such large samples, to produce a measure of how frequently people at various income levels experience certain emotions (like, say, how often people at a certain income have to deal with grief over a lost loved one; and every other possible thing that impacts emotional state).

With this approach, they found what all previous studies found: that once annual income hits a certain point, there are no significant gains in happiness after that. In other words, more money, is no use to us. Not as far as living a life worth living. In fact, this study found that sometimes, more money after that point actually *decreases* life satisfaction! Called "satiation," the income level where this occurs did vary by country and region in general, averaged globally, "the satiation point for life evaluation occurred at approximately $95,000, at roughly 7.58" and "for positive emotions, satiation occurred at a lower level of income ($60,000), as did [the reduction in] negative emotions ($75,000)." In fact, "after satiation had been reached" for the life-satisfaction measure, "further increases in income were associated with slight decrements" to subjective well-being (which they called 'turning points', where increases started to reduce life satisfaction).

In simple words: The American Dream does not make sense. Going for a higher income than § 100 000 a year won't make you happier or add to your life quality. On the contrary, it is likely to influence the life quality of both yourself and others badly.

Isn't it a waste that so many of the most beautiful houses and properties of the world are empty for most of the time, because their owners each have 10 houses each and cannot use them all simultaneously?

I have been a physician for many billionaires, and they don't seem to be much happier than normal people, which the above-mentioned study confirms. Why destroy our planet in the hunt for unlimited wealth for a few families, when no-one is benefiting from it in terms of happiness?

Only slaves have a price tag, and it does not matter if the price tag is one hundred or 100 million dollars. A slave is still a slave.

References Chapter 5

1. Hsin Hsin Ming, the Book of Nothing: Discourses on the Faith Mind of Sosan by Osho Published   September 30th 1983 by Osho International Foundation

2. Andrew Jebb, Louis Tay, Ed Diener, and Shigehiro Oishi, "Happiness, Income Satiation and Turning Points around the World," Nature: Human Behavior 2.1 (January 2018): pp. 33-38.

Illustrations:
https://commons.wikimedia.org/wiki/File:Europe_Boardman_Robinson.jpg

Chapter 6: The Whip

The other side of the slave driver philosophy is the whip. Do as we say, or......

Mankind have become experts in performing all kinds of cruelty including, torture, terror, brainwashing and sadistic rituals in order to keep the slaves in fear.

The culmination is the mosaic religions with their concept of Hell as a place where the sinners and infidels spend eternity being burned and tortured. It is a well-known medical fact that the most terrible pain that can be inflicted on a person is severe burns. In the old times the preachers used to hold someone's hand briefly over a fire in order to demonstrate what would await if he didn't follow the orders from the church.
The mosaic religions also had the concept of original sin, and that we all were born as sinners.

This belief led to an increased amount of anxiety depression and low self confidence among people. Death became something to be feared, and not a natural passage to the spiritual world that was nothing to be afraid of as it is portrayed in most native religions.

It is easier to control a person who is full of guilt and fear of death.

We now live in a death dominated culture. The news is mainly concerned about how many that died in the accident in X, the nature catastrophe in Y and the terror attack, mass shooting or war in Z.

A great deal of all out movies are murder mysteries and contain violent fights, where dozens of people are killed.

My grandfather, Knut Stenborg published a book in 1937 called "in the center of the storm" that was about his first-hand experiences of the Russian Revolution from 1917-1918. He states that the main reason for the collapse of the Socialist Kerensky government that ruled Russia from February to November 1917, after the peaceful overturning of power from Tsar Nikolai II in February, was that Kerensky abolished death penalty in Russia, probably because of good ethical and humanistic reasons.

The result was that a great part of the soldiers in the Russian army deserted and instead started to create havoc on the country side, leading to the chaos and disorder that later was used by the communist Bolshevik party, governed by Vladimir Illich Lenin and his co-criminals, Trotsky and Stalin in order to take the power, supported by Swedish and American Bankers.

The old mosaic religions gave arise to skepticism when people got more educated and started to think more independently.

How can you punish someone in eternity for a crime committed during a limited time?

If God created us and is omnipotent and all-wise, he must have known that many of us didn't have the character to be able to qualify for paradise.

This means that he deliberately created a universe where a majority of the souls will be tormented in eternity. What kind of God is that?

Everyone in Paradise is likely to know someone who ended up in Hell.

Even if your parents sometimes were mean to you, I don't think any child would like their parents to burn in hell forever and be comfortable with that.

If that is the case, even the paradise must be populated with revengeful, non-forgiving and emotionally blocked persons. How can then paradise be a paradise?

Jesus Christ forgave his enemies on the cross and prayed to God "Please forgive them, because they don't know what they do".

On the contrast, God sends the sinners on the day of doom to burn forever in Hell.

How can these two very different personalities be related and be of Father and Son?

Many similar questions and lack of logic in the conventional Mosaic Religions paved the way for atheism and materialism, the belief that has dominated mankind in the west for the last 100 years.

In his book "The Science Delusion"(1) Rupert Sheldrake formulates the "Scientific Creed"

"Here are the ten core beliefs that most scientists take for granted. Everything is essentially mechanical. Dogs, for example, are complex mechanisms, rather than living organisms with goals of their own. Even people are machines, 'lumbering robots', in Richard Dawkins's vivid phrase, with brains that are like genetically programmed computers.

2. All matter is unconscious. It has no inner life or subjectivity or point of view. Even human consciousness is an illusion produced by the material activities of brains.

3. The total amount of matter and energy is always the same (with the exception of the Big Bang, when all the matter and energy of the universe suddenly appeared).

4. The laws of nature are fixed. They are the same today as they were at the beginning, and they will stay the same forever.

5. Nature is purposeless, and evolution has no goal or direction.

6. All biological inheritance is material, carried in the genetic material, DNA, and in other material structures.

7. Minds are inside heads and are nothing but the activities of brains. When you look at a tree, the image of the tree you are seeing is not 'out there', where it seems to be, but inside your brain.

8. Memories are stored as material traces in brains and are wiped out at death.

9. Unexplained phenomena like telepathy are illusory.

10. Mechanistic medicine is the only kind that really works.

Together, these beliefs make up the philosophy or ideology of materialism, whose central assumption is that everything is essentially material or physical, even minds. This belief-system became dominant within science in the late nineteenth century, and is now taken for granted. Many scientists are unaware that materialism is an assumption: they simply think of it as science, or the scientific view of reality, or the scientific worldview. They are not actually taught about it, or given a chance to discuss it. They absorb it by a kind of intellectual osmosis. In everyday usage, materialism refers to a way of life devoted entirely to material interests, a preoccupation with wealth, possessions and luxury. These attitudes are no doubt encouraged by the materialist philosophy, which denies the existence of any spiritual realities or non-material goals"

In this very interesting book, Rupert Sheldrake attacks each of these pseudo-scientific materialistic dogmas with data from modern science and sharp logic.

We are now suffering the consequences from this, with very small concerns for the future of our Planet, as we will only stay her for a short time and then it is over. Who cares anyway? We also believe that we can solve problems by killing people. We just should not get caught. There will be no consequences or karma on a spiritual level.

Despite all the achievements of science and technology, materialism is now facing a credibility crunch that was unimaginable in the twentieth century. The problems of development and consciousness remain unsolved. Many details have been discovered, dozens of genomes have been sequenced, and brain scans are ever more precise. But there is still no proof that life and minds can be explained by physics and chemistry alone and there is no explanation where all the logic and wisdom that can be experienced in evolution comes from.

As the fear of death has been one of the key methods for used by the slave drivers to keep us subservient and obedient, it is very interesting from both a philosophical and political point of view to take a look on what modern science tells us about death and near-death experiences.

Death, a Big Adventure, or the Ultimate Catastrophe?

It is quite interesting to observe that still, a large majority of humanity believes in God or a spiritual force and in life after death, while, for example, Wikipedia constantly favoring a materialistic / atheistic belief as being "scientific" and all forms of faith that our consciousness can exist independently of the body as superstition. "
According to the US Departmen of Statistics www.pewforum.org think 74% of Americans in a life after death, 79% believe in different kinds of miracles, and 92% believe in some kind of God or spiritual force that govern existence.

There is a widespread fear of death in the Western civilization in contrast to many eastern and ancient civilizations. Could it be that this is perhaps the most important reason why the Western culture has been dominant the last centuries?
Another issue related to death is the question of where we come from before we were born? There is reason to believe that there may be similarities between these two states, or is our consciousness just a byproduct of our brain, just like a fart created by our digestive systems, which is the result of a spontaneously created life process evolved from dead matter with the help of natural selection?
We will make a logical analysis of the possible health consequences of the different belief systems and the scientific evidence backing up the different theories.

Near Death Experiences

Wikipedia states(2):

"Since earliest times it has been known that people who are dying or have a near brush with death may report profound and unusual experiences. Interest in these phenomena was largely in the province of religion and parapsychology until 1975, when the medical philosopher Raymond Moody's collection of people's experiences was published. His book, Life

After Life(3), initiated an explosion of popular interest and has since been translated into more than 30 languages. He labelled this complex cluster of subjective changes the Near-Death Experience (NDE).

Up to 2005, 95% of world cultures have been documented making some mention of NDEs. These phenomenon's can include:

- A sense/awareness of being dead.
- A sense of peace, well-being and painlessness. Positive emotions. A sense of removal from the world.
- An out-of-body experience. A perception of one's body from an outside position. Sometimes observing medical professionals performing resuscitation efforts.
- A "tunnel experience" or entering a darkness. A sense of moving up, or through, a passageway or staircase.
- A rapid movement toward and/or sudden immersion in a powerful light (or "Being of Light") which communicates with the person.
- An intense feeling of unconditional love and acceptance.
- Encountering "Beings of Light", "Beings dressed in white", or similar. Also, the possibility of being reunited with deceased loved ones.
- Receiving a life review, commonly referred to as "seeing one's life flash before one's eyes".
- Receiving knowledge about one's life and the nature of the universe.
- Approaching a border, or a decision by oneself or others to return to one's body, often accompanied by a reluctance to return.
- Suddenly finding oneself back inside one's body.

Moody emphasized that this represents a compound picture. In each case there are similarities, yet no two NDEs are identical, nor are all these elements necessarily present, and the sequence may vary. The NDE stages have been noted for their similarity to the so-called hero's journey in literature and psychedelic experiences with drugs like Ketamine, Ayahuasca and Ibogaine. Kenneth Ring (1980) subdivided the NDE on a five-stage continuum. The subdivisions were:

- Peace
- Body separation
- Entering darkness
- Seeing the light
- Entering the light

He stated that 60% experienced stage 1 (feelings of peace and contentment), but only 10% experienced stage 5 ("entering the light"). "

"Clinical circumstances associated with near-death experiences include cardiac arrest in myocardial infarction (clinical death); shock in postpartum loss of blood or in perioperative complications; septic or anaphylactic shock; electrocution; coma resulting from traumatic brain damage; intracerebral hemorrhage or cerebral infarction; attempted suicide; near-drowning or asphyxia; apnea; and serious depression. In contrast to common belief, Kenneth Ring argues that attempted suicides do not lead more often to unpleasant NDEs than unintended near-death situations."
The experiences were shown to be remarkably similar across different cultures and belief systems, i.e., it didn´t matter if the subject of the experience was atheist, Christian, Muslim or Hindu, except for the fact that the Hindus were more likely to meet Hindu religious entities and the Christians figures like Jesus or Mother Mary.
Psychological investigations showed no connection between NDEs and psychiatric conditions and certain personality traits, except for a tendency for an increased capability of recalling dreams. However, it was uncertain if this capability was a result of the NDE or a factor present also before the NDE.

Prevalence

The prevalence of NDEs has been variable in the studies that have been performed. According to the Gallup and Proctor survey in 1980–1981, of a representative sample of the American population, data showed that 15% described themselves as having had an "unusual experience" when on the verge of death or having a "close call".

Berlin sociologist Hubert Knoblauch performed a more selective study in Germany and found that 4% of the sample population had an NDE."

Different theories about the nature of NDEs

Just like people who had a NDE have a tendency to see Jesus in the light if they are Christian, and Krishna if they are Hindu, people who hear about NDEs have a tendency to interpret the NDE phenomenon according to their own language, belief system and cultural context. If they are atheist, they claim that NDEs is a result of biochemical reactions in a dying brain, if they are religiously inclined, NDEs are seen as a proof that there is life after death. What seems pretty clear though, is that almost everyone who had a near death experience him/herself had a profound change in their way of looking at life and are no longer afraid of death. For them, the experience was so strong, they no longer doubt there is an afterlife.

Kenneth Ring (4)(professor of psychology) has identified a consistent set of value and belief changes associated with people who have had a near-death experience. Among these changes one finds a greater appreciation for life, higher self-esteem, greater compassion for others, less concern for acquiring material wealth, a heightened sense of purpose and self-understanding, desire to learn, elevated spirituality, greater ecological sensitivity and planetary concern, and a feeling of being more intuitive. Changes may also include increased physical sensitivity; diminished tolerance of light, alcohol, and drugs; a feeling that the brain has been "altered" to encompass more; and a feeling that one is now using the "whole brain" rather than a small part. Some people also got inspiration for new inventions, scientific discoveries and solutions to different kind of personal problems during their NDE. However, not all after-effects are beneficial and Greyson describes circumstances where changes in attitudes and behavior can lead to psychosocial and psychospiritual problems. Often the problems are those of the adjustment to ordinary life in the wake of the NDE, i.e. perceiving they have to change their life in order to encompass their new insights, which is not always an easy thing.

The core issue is: Is consciousness simply a result of brain activities or can consciousness exist independently of the brain?

Below is a summary of the arguments for an afterlife explanation:

Argument 1: People have NDEs while they are brain dead

"Dr. Michael Sabom is a cardiologist whose book entitled Light and Death includes a detailed medical and scientific analysis of an amazing near-death experience of a woman named Pam Reynolds. She underwent a rare operation to remove a giant basilar artery aneurysm in her brain that threatened her life. The size and location of the aneurysm, however, precluded its safe removal using the standard neuro-surgical techniques. She was referred to a doctor who had pioneered a daring surgical procedure known as hypothermic cardiac arrest. It allowed Pam's aneurysm to be excised with a reasonable chance of success. This operation, nicknamed "standstill" by the doctors who perform it, required that Pam's body temperature be lowered to 60 degrees Fahrenheit, her heartbeat and breathing stopped, her brain waves flattened, and the blood drained from her head. In everyday terms, she was put to death. After removing the aneurysm, she was restored to life. During the time that Pam was in standstill, she experienced an NDE. Her remarkably detailed veridical out-of-body observations during her surgery were later verified to be true. Her case is considered to be one of the strongest cases of veridical (i.e., verified) evidence in NDE research because of her ability to describe the unique surgical instruments, the surgical procedures used on her, and her ability to describe in detail these events while she was clinically brain dead. "

Argument 2: Out-of-body perception during NDEs have been verified

Dr. Bruce Greyson documented the following case: Al Sullivan was a 55-year-old truck driver who was undergoing triple by-pass surgery in 1988 when he had a powerful NDE including an encounter with his deceased mother and brother-in-law, who told Al to go back to tell one of his neighbors their son with lymphoma will live. Furthermore, during the NDE, Sullivan accurately noticed the surgeon, Dr. Hiroyoshi Takata, operating on him was "flapping his arms as if trying to fly" with his hands in his armpits. When he came back to his body after the surgery was over, Sullivan's cardiologist was startled that Sullivan could describe Dr. Takata's habit of arm flapping. It was Dr. Takata's idiosyncratic method of keeping his hands sterile and pointing out to surgical instruments and giving instructions to surgical staff. There are many similar reports. If you want to read more, we recommend you to Read Dr Moody's book.

Argument 3. People born blind can see during an NDE

In their article: Near Death and Out-of-Body Experiences in the Blind: A

Study of Apparent Eyeless Vision, Dr. Kenneth Ring and Dr. Sharon Cooper(5) reported:

"Our findings revealed that blind persons, including those blind from birth, do report classic NDEs of the kind common to sighted persons; that the great preponderance of blind persons claim to see during NDEs and OBEs; and that occasionally claims of visually-based knowledge that could not have been obtained by normal means can be independently corroborated. "

"Vicki was born very prematurely, having been in the womb only 22 weeks at delivery, and weighed just three pounds at birth. After- ward, her weight dropped precariously to one pound, 14 ounces. As was common for premature babies in the 1950s, she was placed in an airlock incubator through which oxygen was administered. Unfortunately, because of a failure to regulate the concentration of oxygen properly, Vicki was given too much and, along with about 50,000 other premature babies born in the United States about the same time, suffered such optic nerve damage as to leave her completely blind. As she made clear in an initial interview with another researcher, Greg Wilson, who kindly provided his tapes and transcripts to us, she has never had any visual experience whatever, nor does she even understand the nature of light:

In early 1973, Vicki, then 22, was working as an occasional singer in a nightclub in Seattle. One night, at closing time, she was unable to call for a taxi to drive her home and circumstances forced her to take the only other option: a ride with a couple of inebriated patrons. Not surprisingly, a serious accident ensued during which Vicki was thrown out of their van. Her injuries were extensive and life-threatening, and included a skull fracture and concussion, and damage to her neck, back, and one leg. In fact, it took her a full year after being released from the hospital before she could stand upright with- out the risk of fainting.

Vicki clearly remembers the frightening prelude to the crash itself, but she has only a hazy recall of finding herself alternately out of her body and then back inside of it at the accident scene. Her only definite recollection of anything external to herself while out-of-body is a very brief glimpse of the crumpled vehicle. Although this aspect of her experience was confusing, she does claim that while in her out-of-body state she was aware of being in a nonphysical body that had a distinct form and that was, as she put it, "like it was made of light."

She has no memory of her trip to Harborview Hospital in the ambulance, but after she arrived at the emergency room, she came again to awareness when she found herself up on the ceiling watching a male doctor and a woman—she is not sure whether the woman was another physician or a nurse—working on her body. She could overhear their conversation, too, which had to do with their fear that because of possible damage to Vicki's eardrum, she could become deaf as well as blind. Vicki tried desperately to communicate to them that she was fine, but naturally drew no response. She was also aware of seeing her body below her, which she recognized by certain identifying features, such as a distinctive wedding ring she was wearing.

According to her testimony, Vicki first had a very fleeting image of herself lying on the metal table and she was sure, she said, that "it was me," although it took her a moment to register that fact with certainty. As she later told us:

I knew it was me. ... I was pretty thin then. I was quite tall and thin at that point. And I recognized at first that it was a body, but I didn't even know that it was mine initially. Then I perceived that I was up on the ceiling, and I thought, "Well, that's kind of weird. What am I doing up here?" I thought, "Well, this must be me. Am I dead?. . . . " I just briefly saw this body, and ... I knew that it was mine because I wasn't in mine. Then I was just away from it. It was that quick.

Almost immediately after that, as she recalls, she found herself going up through the ceilings of the hospital until she was above the roof of the building itself, during which time she had a brief panoramic view of her surroundings. She felt very exhilarated during this ascension and enjoyed tremendously the freedom of movement she was experiencing. She also began to hear sublimely beautiful and exquisitely harmonious music akin to the sound of wind chimes.

With scarcely a noticeable transition, she then discovered she had been sucked head-first into a tube and felt that she was being pulled up into it. The enclosure itself was dark, Vicki said, yet she was aware that she was moving toward light. As she reached the opening of the tube, the music that she had heard earlier seemed to be transformed into hymns, similar to those she heard during her previous NDE, and she then "rolled out" to find herself lying on grass.

She was surrounded by trees and flowers and a vast number of people. She was in a place of tremendous light, and the light, Vicki said, was something you could feel as well as see. What the light conveyed was love. Even the people she saw were bright and reflected the light of this love. "Everybody there was made of light. And I was made of light. There was love everywhere. It was like love came from the grass, love came from the birds, love came from the trees."

In the midst of this rapture, Vicki was suddenly overcome with a sense of total knowledge:

I had a feeling like I knew everything . . . and like everything made sense. I just knew that this was where . . . this place was where I would find the answers to all the questions about life, and about the planets, and about God, and about everything. . . . It's like the place was the knowing.

And then she was indeed flooded with information of a religious nature as well as scientific and mathematical knowledge. She came to understand languages she didn't know. All this overwhelmed and astonished her:

I don't know beans about math and science. ... I all of a sudden understood intuitively almost things about calculus, and about the way planets were made. And I don't know anything about that. . . . I felt there was nothing I didn't know.

As these revelations were unfolding, Vicki noticed that now next to her was a figure whose radiance was far greater than the illumination of any of the persons she had so far encountered. Immediately, she recognized this being to be Jesus, for she had seen him once before, during her previous NDE. He greeted her tenderly, while she conveyed her excitement to him about her newfound omniscience and her joy at being there and with him again.

Telepathically, he communicated to her: "Isn't it wonderful? Everything is beautiful here, and it fits together. And you'll find that. But you can't stay here now. It's not your time to be here yet and you have to go back."

Vicki reacted, understandably enough, with extreme disappointment and protested vehemently, "No, I want to stay with you." But the being reassured her that she would come back, but for now, she had to "go back and learn and teach more about loving and forgiving."

Still resistant, however, Vicki then learned that she also needed to go back to have her children. With that, Vicki, who was then childless but who "desperately wanted" to have children—and who has since given birth to three—became almost eager to return and finally consented.

However, before Vicki could leave, the being said to her, in these exact words, "But first, watch this."

And what Vicki then saw was "everything from my birth" in a complete panoramic review of her life, and as she watched, the being gently commented to help her understand the significance of her actions and their repercussions.

The last thing Vicki remembers, once the life review had been completed, are the words, "You have to leave now. "She then experienced "a sickening thud" like a roller-coaster going backwards, and found herself back in her body, feeling heavy and full of pain."

"Another case came from a woman interviewed in the early 1980s but Dr Kenneth Ring, who was 48 years old at the time (5). She had had her NDE in connection with a surgical procedure in 1974. What was especially noteworthy about her account at the outset, however, was her mention of her unusually garbed anesthesiologist. As she explained, he was a physician who often worked with children. And because he had found that his young patients often were confused by a team of similarly clad green garmented doctors, he had taken to wearing a yellow surgical hat with magenta butterflies on it so he, at least, could easily be recognized. All this will, of course, be highly relevant to this woman's account of her experience which will now be described in her own words. She had gone into shock when she heard her physician exclaim, "This woman's dying!" At that point:

Bang, I left! The next thing I was aware of was floating on the ceiling. And seeing down there, with his hat on his head, I knew who he was because of the hat on his head [i.e., the anesthesiologist with the magenta butterfly cap]. . . it was so vivid. I'm very nearsighted, too, by the way, which was another one of the startling things that happened to me when I left my body. I see at fifteen feet what most people see at four hundred. . . . They were hooking me up to a machine that was behind my head. And my very first thought was, "Jesus, I can see! I can't believe it, I can see!" I could read the numbers on the machine behind my head and I was just so thrilled. And I thought, "They gave me back my glasses. . . ." (Ring, 1984, p. 42)

She went on to describe further details of her operation, including how her body looked, the shaving of her belly, and various medical procedures that her surgical team were performing upon her, and then found herself looking at another object from a position high above her physical body:

"From where I was looking, I could look down on this enormous fluorescent light . . . and it was so dirty on top of the light. [Could you see the top of the light fixture?] Yes, and it was filthy. And I remember thinking, "Got to tell the nurses about that.""

Ring concluded that:

"Whether one is blind from birth, loses one's sight in later life, or suffers from severe visual impairment, the type of NDE reported appears to be much the same and is not structurally different from those described by sighted persons. "

"Of our 21 NDErs in blind people, 15 claimed to have had some kind of sight, three were not sure whether they saw or not, and the remaining three did not appear to see at all. All but one of those who either denied or were unsure about being able to see came from those who were blind from birth, which means that only half of the NDErs in that category stated unequivocally that they had distinct visual impressions during their experience. Nevertheless, it is not clear by any means whether those respondents blind from birth who claimed not to have seen were in fact unable to, or simply failed to recognize what seeing was. For instance, one man whom we classified as a non-visualizer told us that he could not explain how he had the perceptions he did because "I don't know what you mean by 'seeing.'" He was not the only such person to admit such perplexity, so that even among those cases we felt obliged to classify as not involving sight, the possibility is not entirely foreclosed. As a whole, however, our data here are quite consistent in indicating that the preponderance of our blind NDErs do indeed report vision during their near-death encounters, while only a minority are unsure about the matter or, in some cases, have no clear sense of sight."

"One fairly obvious possibility that has often been advanced in connection with the NDEs and OBEs of sighted persons is that this experience is some kind of a dream, perhaps a lucid or exceptionally vivid dream, which has such realistic properties that it is easily mis- interpreted and thus given an ontological status it does not deserve. To evaluate this hypothesis, we first need to inquire into what is known about normal oneiric processes(=dreams) in the blind. Fortunately, there has been a great deal of research devoted to the dreams of the blind, some of it going back more than a hundred years. As a result of these investigations, certain generalizations about the presence of visual imagery in dreams appear to stand up quite well. Among these "empirical cornerstones" are that there are no visual images in the dreams of the congenitally blind; individuals blinded before the age of 5 also tend not to have visual imagery; those who become sightless between the age of 5 to 7 may or may not retain visual imagery; and most persons who lose their sight after age 7 do retain visual imagery, although its clarity tends to fade with time. In addition, various researchers have found that audition tends to be the primary sense involved in dreams of the blind, with tactile and kinesthetic elements next. "

Dr Rings conclusion is that "this is not simple "vision" at all as we are wont to understand it, but almost a kind of seeming omniscience that completely transcends what mere seeing could ever afford. Indeed, what we appear to have here is a distinctive state of consciousness, which we would like to call *transcendental awareness.* In this type of awareness, it is not of course that the eyes see anything; it is rather that the mind itself sees, but more in the sense of "understanding" or "taking in" than of visual perception as such. Or alternatively, we might say that it is not the eye that sees, but the "I."

It is also extremely interesting to note that" people who surgically regain their sight take some time to learn visual identification of objects, the initial OBEs in the congenitally blind should exhibit the same property if the experience depends upon the visual pathways of the nervous system." (6)

Argument 4: Persons being able to communicate to others while they have an NDE

An anecdotal example of evidence that a person's consciousness leaves and returns to their body during an NDE comes from the research of Dr. Melvin Morse. Olga Gearhardt was a 63-year-old woman who underwent a heart transplant because of a severe virus that attacked her heart tissue. Her entire family awaited at the hospital during the surgery, except for her son-in-law, who stayed home. The transplant was a success, but at exactly 2:15 am, her new heart stopped beating. It took the frantic transplant team three more hours to revive her. Her family was only told in the morning that her operation was a success, without other details. When they called her son-in-law with the good news, he had his own news to tell. He had already learned about the successful surgery. At exactly 2:15 am, while he was sleeping, he awoke to see his Olga, his mother-in-law, at the foot of his bed. She told him not to worry, that she was going to be alright. She asked him to tell her daughter (his wife). He wrote down the message, and the time of day and then fell asleep. Later on at the hospital, Olga regained consciousness. Her first words were "did you get the message?" She was able to confirm that she left her body during her near-death experience and was able to travel to her son-in-law to communicate to him the message. This anecdotal evidence demonstrates that the near-death experience is a return to consciousness at the point of death, when the brain is dying. Dr. Melvin Morse thoroughly researched Olga's testimony and every detail had objective verification including the scribbled note by the son-in-law."

Argument 5: Out-of-body experiences have been validated in scientific studies

Dr. Charles Tart, www.issc-taste.org and www.paradigm-sys.com, is a transpersonal psychologist and parapsychologist known for his psychological work on the nature of consciousness (particularly altered states of consciousness), as one of the founders of the field of transpersonal psychology, and for his research in scientific parapsychology.

The following is an excerpt from an article by Dr. Tart which was published in the Journal of the American Society for Psychical Research. In it, Dr. Tart documents the out-of-body experience of a young woman who was one of his research subjects. What makes this particular out-of-body experience remarkable is that she was able to leave her physical body and read a 5-digit number, which was at a significant distance, and correctly give it to him upon return. The odds of guessing a 5-digit number correctly are 1 in 100,000. Her OBE a good example of "veridical perception" where verified events are observed while in an out-of-body state.(7)

Argument 6: NDEs induce profound positive changes in the personality and sometimes profound instances of miraculous healing:

Pim van Lommel(4) and many others have noted profound positive changes in personality and social attitudes after an NDE. Below are these changes documented in a group who had an NDE after a cardiac arrest compared with a control group who had a cardiac arrest without a NDE from

Table 4.
Significant differences in life-change inventory-scores of patients with and
without NDE at 2-year follow-up

LIfe-change inventory questionnaire	p
Social attitude	
Showing own feelings	0·034
Acceptance of others*	0·012
More loving, empathic*	0·002
Understanding others*	0·003
Involvement in family*	0·008
Religious attitude	
Understand purpose of life*	0·020
Sense inner meaning of life*	0·028
Interest in spirituality*	0·035
Attitude to death	
Fear of death*	0·009
Belief in life after death*	0·007
Others	
Interest in meaning of life	0·020
Understanding oneself	0·019
Appreciation of ordinary things	0·0001

Dr Melvin Morse concluded after following up on children under 15 who had a NDE "Adults who had NDEs gave more money to charity than control subjects, volunteered in the community, were in helping professions, did not suffer from drug abuse, use many over-the-counter medications, and ate more fresh fruit and vegetables than control populations. He also found that they often could not wear watches as they would mysteriously break, and often had electrical conduction problems such as shorting out lap top computers and erasing credit cards."

Here comes an impressive example from Dr Braghettas research group in Brazil:

"Our case was a 45-year-old male born in the state of Minas Gerais, southeastern Brazil. He reported having committed his fist "cruelty" at 9 years of age, when he put fire to his brother's genitals. After that, he got involved with theft and robbery, became a drug dealer and drug user, and was prostituted. He tried to kill his parents because of disagreements. He was institutionalized at Fundacão CASA (for minors). When he turned 19, he was sentenced to 44 years in prison for four homicides and drug trafficking.

After 3 years in prison, when he was 22, he was attacked by other prisoners for revenge. He was stabbed 14 times. This attack caused diaphragmatic rupture and affected several other organs. He was referred to an emergency unit and submitted to surgery.

Later, the prisoner reported to have had a spiritual experience during surgery, where he saw himself descending into the depths of hell. Then, a "divine hand" removed him from that place and lifted him up into the air. He could see himself lying on the operating table, with several doctors around him. The "hand" carried him further up until reaching a certain height, way above the city. While he was up amid clouds, he reported seeing several lights and "a golden city." He manifested a desire to go there, but a voice told him that "he was not ready because he had a mission to accomplish." Then, the "hand" brought him back to his body. He was later surprised to be alive.

After that experience, he reported to have changed his view of life. He regretted his crimes and became involved with religion and spirituality. He also reported a situation in which a former enemy (a man who had tried to kill him several times) was imprisoned. He offered himself to stay in the same cell as his enemy. Contrary to expectations, he did not attack his enemy.

After 26 years in prison, he was granted conditional release in 2010. He now lives in the metropolitan region of São Paulo, lives with a partner since January 2011, has four children, and attends a Baptist church. He plans to make progress and build a home where he can live with his family. He believes that his mission is to help the next of kin through his life history."

Near-death experiences have cured people from cancer and blindness:

Dr. Kenneth Ring also documented the case of Ralph Duncan who died of leukemia and had an NDE. During his NDE, Jesus cured him and told him he no longer had leukemia. Duncan returned from death cancer-free. (Howard Mikel). Another case involves a woman by the name of Anita Moorjani who was completely cured from her Stage IV cancer after her NDE. Doctors at the hospital had given Anita just hours to live when she arrived at the hospital, unable to move as a result of the cancer ravaging her body for over three years. Anita shares her experience of entering another dimension and being given a choice of whether to return to life or not in her book entitled "Dying to Be Me: My Journey from Cancer, to Near Death, to True Healing."(9)

A near-death experience cured a person's congenital blindness:
A blind and mute 67-year-old diabetic woman with severe heart problems was about to undergo open-heart surgery when a Being of Light appeared and healed her of all her illnesses. The cardiologists could offer no explanation for her cure. (4)

You might say that having a near death experience seems to be one of the most efficient and well documented treatment methods ever documented by medical science, although it is hard to systemize and reproduce.
This also demonstrates that fear of death has a detrimental effect on both our health and our social behavior and that a culture dominated by a positive approach to death is likely be more successful than the current mainstream culture.
If the scientific data presented earlier in this chapter are true, death seems to be something that we really can look forward to, more like going on vacation instead of something to be afraid of and resist.

My father Kurt Nordfors was a teacher at the end of his career, and he was buried the same day as the school holidays started in Sweden, accompanied by the traditional Swedish psalm that always used to be performed at Swedish graduations, "The Flowering Time is Coming". It was a very beautiful moment, filled with bliss and joy...

A society that has a positive view on life and death is likely to be dominated by pessimism, oppression and dictatorship. It is simply harder to dominate people who are not afraid of death

However, there is something else that has been in development through history that brings with it the solution to tyranny and oppression, a sort of divine intervention: democracy.

References Chapter 6:

1. Sheldrake, Rupert:

The Science Delusion: Freeing the Spirit of Enquiry
ISBN: 9781444727920
2. https://en.wikipedia.org/wiki/Near-death_experience
3. Life After Life: The Investigation of a Phenomenon---Survival of Bodily Death ISBN 1452631700
by Raymond A. Moody Jr. M.D. (Author), Dick Hill (Narrator)
4. Lessons from the Light: What We Can Learn from the NDE (2006) - By Kenneth Ring ISBN-10: 0306459833
5. https://digital.library.unt.edu/ark:/67531/metadc799333/m2/1/high_res_d/vol16-no2-101.pdf
6. Journal of Near-Death Studies, 16(12) Waiter 199? © 1997 Human Sciences Press. Inc.
7. http://www.aspr.com/jaspr.htm
8. Near-death experience in survivors of cardiac arrest: a prospective study in the Netherlands
Pim van Lommel, Ruud van Wees, Vincent Meyers, Ingrid Elfferich, Lancet 2001; 358: 2039–45 Lancet 2001

9. Dying To Be Me: My Journey from Cancer, to Near Death, to True Healing." Anita Morjani. Hay House Inc.; 1 edition (September 1, 2014)ISBN-10: 1401937535

Illustration: "Lux Eterna" Oil Painting Performed by Helen Nordfors.

Chapter 7: Democracy.

Do you consult a doctor or a crowd when you are sick?

What is democracy? The rule of the people – but who are the people, what do they rule over and how do they rule over it? The political scientist Robert Dahl has proposed this definition – the ideal of the democracy is:

1. Political equality for the people.

2. Effective part-taking by the people.

3. Wide political understanding by the people.

4. Control of the political agenda by the people.

5. "The people" is as inclusive as it can be (people who have permanent stay in a country and have a certain age).

This has never been the case in the world, ever. Not for a single state. However, it will hopefully be the case by the introduction of Demosocracy, which is direct, deliberative and participatory. The people's will, the result and the justification are all maximized in this new system.

Why this is your solution no matter your ideology:

Society has problems, these problems pave the way for problem solutions, or ideologies.

An ideology is considered to have the following properties according to the researcher Ronald Inglehart:(1)

1. An ideology a problem to solve, or an enemy.

2. It has to find a methodology to solve that problem .

3. This solution has to be understandable by the participants.

4. The extreme parts have an extreme process to force people into the ideology.

5. There is a leadership towards a goal.

6. It is collectivistic in nature.

7. It makes you aware that the enemy is observing at all times.

The ideology is a narrative about some groups fight for freedom that is acted upon by a group (they are not always the same). The big problems in society that have the consciousness and material needs fulfilled create popular movements. The movements get leaderships.

Marxism tells the story about class-war, the workers emancipation, the employers are the enemy, the workers method is organizing and doing actions that revolve around work.

Feminism tells the story about women's fight, the women's emancipation, the patriarchy is the enemy, the women's method is organizing and doing actions that revolve around women.

The list of ideologies goes on...

As the means of production change, the material basis of society changes, the economy. Ibn Khaldun (2) (one of the fathers of sociology) predicted that when a society gets new technology, the leaders and popular movements get their goals out of line. In the information era today, this is very true. The political parties use statistics about opinions and change their rhetoric's accordingly instead of trying to change opinions. This is not good for the movements.

Which ideology could solve this problem? The democratic one of course.

Democratic positivists tell the story about the peoples fight, the people's emancipation, the anti-democratic principles, or tyranny, which are the enemy, the ultimate method of the democratic positivists will most likely be Demosocracy.

Democratic behavior on an organizational level is reached this way, and on individual levels it is reached by maturity, cooperation in communication and taking responsibility for the common good.

The point is: when we get new technology, our society gets into a crisis, leaders do not help the people who organize in the old ideologies anymore - therefore they need to change into either more democracy or less.

Marshall McLuhan(3) explained that society will be dominated by the kind go communication media that is used. The tribal societies were dominated by verbal communication, the kingdoms with written laws. The next stage was the printed word that gave rise to the scientific revolution, common schooling and representative democracy. The next step will be the digital age, and we believe that 'Liquid Democracy and Demosocracy will be the next major step.

The history of democracy:

In the hunter-gathering societies it was common that every adult could influence group decisions. Such an egalitarian approach is familiar to anthropologists, studying the customs of small tribal groups, but it has unfortunately been a rarity in more developed societies. We believe it is part of human nature to make decisions together, but also to somehow delegate some of the decisions to people you know personally and trust, just like in the type of tribe we have been living in during most of our human evolution, where everyone had a personal relationship with each tribe member. Primitive Democracy is therefore the natural state of humanity. (4)

Experience from many indigenous cultures, including my several visits to Western Samoa, shows that the persons acquiring the highest ranking and respect in these societies seldom are the best manipulators and psychopaths, but the people who have been shown to contribute the most to the well-being of the tribe. In Samoa, you gain popularity by arranging good ceremonies and festivities giving the greatest gifts to the tribe. If someone builds a big house with a big fence around for himself, where no-one else has access is simply unthinkable, and if it happens, he will be considered to be mentally ill. and will be excluded from the tribe.

There are some signs of democratic elements in ancient India and pre-Babylonian Mesopotamia. (4)

Athenian Democracy:

94

Athens in the 4th to 5th century BCE had an extraordinary system of government, whereby all male citizens had equal political rights, freedom of speech, and the opportunity to participate directly in the political arena. Further, not only did citizens participate in a direct democracy whereby they themselves made the decisions by which they lived, but they also actively served in the institutions that governed them, and so they directly controlled all parts of the political process, although slaves and women had no voting rights. (5)

Athens emerged in the 7th century BCE, like many other city states, with a dominating powerful aristocracy. (6) However, this domination led to exploitation, creating significant economic, political, and social problems. These problems were exacerbated early in the 6th century; and, as "the many were enslaved too the few, the people rose against the notables". At the same time, a number of popular revolutions disrupted traditional aristocracies. This included Sparta in the second half of the 7th century BCE. Sparta's constitutional reforms introduced a soldier-based state that showed, in turn, how inherited governments can be changed and lead to military victory. After a period of unrest between the rich and poor, Athenians of all classes turned to philosopher Solon to act as a mediator between rival factions, and reached a generally satisfactory solution to their problems. (6)

Solon attempted to satisfy all sides by alleviating the suffering of the poor majority without removing all the privileges of the rich minority.

Overall, the reforms of the lawgiver Solon in 594 BC were devised to avert the political, economic, and moral decline in archaic Athens and gave Athens its first comprehensive code of law.

Even though the Solonian reorganization of the constitution improved the economic position of the Athenian lower classes, it did not eliminate the bitter aristocratic contentions for control of the archonship, the chief executive post. Peisistratus became tyrant of Athens three times and remained in power until his death in 527 BCE.

After the fall of tyranny and before the year 508–507 was over, Cleisthenes proposed a complete reform of the system of government, which later was approved by the popular Ecclesia.

Cleisthenes reorganized the population into ten tribes, with the aim to change the basis of political organization from the family loyalties to political ones, and improve the army's organization.

He also introduced the principle of equality of rights for all, by expanding access to power to more citizens. (6)

This system was comprised of three separate institutions: the Ekklesia, a sovereign governing body that wrote laws and dictated foreign policy; the Boule, a council of representatives from the ten Athenian tribes; and the Dikasteria, the popular courts in which citizens argued cases before a group of lottery-selected jurors. Although this Athenian democracy would survive for only two centuries, Cleisthenes' invention was one of ancient Greece's most enduring contributions to the modern world.(6) The Athenian Democracy was only open to free males more than 18 years old, meaning that only about 40 000 of the entire population of the roughly 100 000 free citizens and 150 000 slaves and 10 000 foreigners were allowed to participate

The Ekklesia:

Athenian democracy was made up of three important institutions. The first was the Ekklesia, or Assembly, the sovereign governing body of Athens. Any member of the demos–any one of those 40,000 adult male citizens–was welcome to attend the meetings of the Ekklesia, which were held 40 times per year in a hillside auditorium west of the Acropolis called the Pnyx. At the meetings, the Ekklesia made decisions about war and foreign policy, wrote and revised laws and approved or condemned the conduct of public officials. The group made decisions by simple majority vote.

The Boule:

The second important institution was the Boule, or Council of Five Hundred. The Boule was a group of 500 men, 50 from each of ten Athenian tribes, who served on the Council for one year. Unlike the Ekklesia, the Boule met every day and did most of the hands-on work of governance. It supervised government workers and was in charge of things like navy ships (triremes) and army horses. It dealt with ambassadors and representatives from other city-states. Its main function was to decide what matters would come before the Ekklesia. In this way, the 500 members of the Boule dictated how the entire democracy would work.

Positions on the Boule were chosen by lot and not by election. This was because, in theory, a random lottery was more democratic than an election: pure chance, after all, could not be influenced by things like money or popularity. The lottery system also prevented the establishment of a permanent class of civil servants who might be tempted to use the government to advance or enrich themselves. (6)

The Dikasteria:

The third important institution was the popular courts, or Dikasteria. Every day, more than 500 jurors were chosen by lot from a pool of male citizens older than 30. Of all the democratic institutions, Aristotle argued that the Dikasteria "contributed most to the strength of democracy" because the jury had almost unlimited power. There were no police in Athens, so it was the demos themselves who brought court cases, argued for the prosecution and the defense, and delivered verdicts and sentences by majority rule.

The End of Athenian Democracy:

Democracy, which had prevailed during Athens' Golden Age, was replaced by a system of oligarchy after the disastrous Athenian defeat in Sicily in 409 BCE. The constitutional change, according to Thucydides, seemed the only way to win much-needed support from Persia against the old enemy Sparta and, further, it was thought that the change would not be a permanent one. Nevertheless, democracy in a slightly altered form did eventually return to Athens and, in any case, the Athenians had already done enough in creating their political system to eventually influence subsequent civilizations two millennia later.

Democracy in ancient Athens was a unique and truly revolutionary system that realized its basic principle to an unprecedented and quite extreme extent: no polis had ever dared to give all its citizens equal political rights, regardless of their descent, wealth, social standing, education, personal qualities, and any other factors that usually determined status in a community.

Ideals such as these would form the cornerstones of all democracies in the modern world. The ancient Greeks have provided us with fine art, breath-taking temples, timeless theatre, and some of the greatest philosophers, but it is democracy which is, perhaps, their greatest and most enduring legacy.

This golden period in History, which in many ways can be seen as the foundation of western civilization, science and philosophy with names as Platon, Socrates, Aristotle, Pythagoras, Archimedes, Aristophanes and Hippocrates are a living proof of the formula, $C + D \rightarrow S^*$, where C is Consciousness level, Culture Creativity, Critical thinking and Courage, D is degree of Democratic Development and S is degree of Successful Society (these formulas will be returned to later on in the book).

* (the symbol + = and)

Democracy increases the moral, cultural, philosophic and scientific level of society and vice versa.

The Athenian Example also shows how democracy continuously needs to be defended, and that the biggest threat against democracy is tyranny and war.

After the shining example of Ancient Greek, more autocratic ruling systems took over.

In various societies, during the long gap between Athenian and modern democracy, the people acquired some elements of democratic power without achieving the ultimate control implicit in the ballot box.

A major problem with the conquering cultures was that countries tended to get bigger and bigger, meaning it was hard to have direct democracy with all the people assembling in the central square, deciding issues by raising their hands, while the traveling distances were too big, and the squares too small to fit millions of individuals. The solution to this problem was representative democracy, where the eligible voters choose a representative that can travel to the democratic assembly.

The Roman Democracy:

The Roman republic, one of the first major conquering cultures, is a good example. Early in the 5th century BC, the citizens of Rome, by a program of passive disobedience, won the right to elect their own officials - the tribunes. Two centuries later, in 287 BC, the decisions of the people's assembly are technically given the status of law. But in this oligarchic society, the votes of the people were mainly important as an expression of the power of their elected tribunes - who themselves become key figures within the oligarchy.

The votes of the Roman people, or plebs, were registered not individually but as the decision of a tribe. Every Roman citizen was a member of a tribe (he was allotted to one, if not a citizen by birth). By the 3rd century BC the number of tribes grew to thirty-five, as more were added to enroll an urban population of new citizens.

When an assembly was called, any citizen could attend. The area of the assembly was divided by ropes into a section for each tribe, and a walkway from each section lead to the presiding magistrate's platform.

Until 139 BC, citizens vote orally, giving their answer to a teller. Thereafter they did mark a tablet and place it in an urn, constituting a secret ballot. When each tribe's returns had been counted, the result was taken to the magistrate as a single vote.

It was the beginning of the kind of voting system needed in any democracy larger than an ancient Greek city (similar methods are now used for elections in many representative democracies).

The Roman Republic was therefore the first government in the western world to have a representative government, despite taking the form of a direct government in the Roman assemblies. The Roman model of governance inspired many political thinkers over the centuries, and today's modern representative democracies imitate more the Roman than the Greek models.

The change from republic to empire, in the 1st century BC, brings a temporary end to democracy in Rome.

The Christian empire, from the 4th century AD, was no more interested than the Roman empire in the opinions of the people. And when the Germanic tribes from the north usurped the western Roman empire, their warrior traditions throw the emphasis more on the hero than the common man.

But in the extreme north, in Scandinavia, there was an interesting example of a kind of a democracy more common among very small and primitive communities. It took place in a thing.

A thing was a meeting of all the free men of a community (several communities coming together for a joint meeting on larger issues constitute an all-thing). The function of these democratic gatherings was limited, for they were legislative rather than political. The free men gather either to affirm or to amend the existing state of the tribal law, which was expounded to them by experts in the matter.

The ancient tradition of the thing is echoed today in the names of the parliaments of Iceland (Althing), Norway (Storting) and Denmark (Folketing).

In northern Italy, some democracy was achieved in the co called communes, the most successful one where in Florence, Pisa and Venice, although it developed more into an Oligarchy, where the rich families had most of the power. A similar system was also applied in Flanders (Belgium, Holland).

It is interesting to note that these semi democratic tendencies coincide with great achievements in science and art, with personalities like Leonardo Da Vinci Michelangelo, Rubens and Rembrandt.

Swiss Democracy:

The forest districts of Switzerland, smaller than other political units in the Middle Ages, adopted a form of government in the Athenian tradition of direct democracy.

These districts were similar to Athens, in that the community was small enough for every adult male to be able to walk to an assembly and cast a vote. In Switzerland such a meeting is called a Landsgemeinde (district community); the earliest record of one is in Schwyz in 1294. Held in the open air, assemblies of this kind become the highest legislative authority in the rural cantons of the Swiss federation - Uri, Schwyz, Unterwalden, Zug, Glarus and Appenzell (13).

The Parliament

The idea of parliament, a place for speaking (from the French parlor) began to evolve from the 12th century in the monarchies of western Europe. It developed from the curia Regis, or 'council of the king', the feudal court in which the monarch made legal judgements and discussed important issues of state with the most powerful bishops and nobles of his kingdom.

A parliament was summoned whenever the king required it. At a period when a monarch was almost permanently on the move to maintain his authority, a parliament would be held wherever the royal court may happen to be.

In the strict hierarchy of medieval society three groups of people stood out as exercising special power. They were the clergy, the nobility and the rich burgesses or burghers (in French bourgeois) of the rapidly developing boroughs, towns and cities. These groups were together known as the three estates.

An interesting exception, at least in principle, was Sweden. Popular opposition to royal pretensions in the mid-15th century led to a unique form of parliament, the "Riksdag", which had representatives from four estates. The fourth estate, after the clergy, nobles and burghers, were the peasants - reflecting the part played by the common people in recent upheavals (4).

A European parliament which exercised unusual power from the early 16th century was the Sejm ('assembly') of Poland.

In 1400-1500 three events changed the C factor (Consciousness, Culture, Courage) enormously, making ground for the development of democracy. One was the development of universities, where knowledge was published and shared, instead of being kept secret by individual alchemists and researchers, and the other two came from Germany, Johannes Gutenberg and Martin Luther.

In the middle of the 15th century, Johannes Gutenberg started the Printing Revolution, which is widely regarded as the most important invention of the second millennia. (8)

These events had a tremendous impact on the development of written language and the general education level, with the consequence of increasing demands for democracy and freedom for the people, leading to social tensions and revolutions, the most famous ones in England 1640-1660 and in France (1789-99).

In 1628 the Parliament of England passed the Petition of Right. It established, among other things, the illegality of taxation without parliamentary consent and of arbitrary imprisonment. The idea of the political party with factions took form in Britain around the time of the English Civil War (1642–1651) (10).

In France, the Declaration of the Rights of Man and of the Citizen adopted on 26 August 1789 declared that "Men are born and remain free and equal in rights" and proclaimed the universal character of human rights. Universal male suffrage was established for the election of the National Convention in September 1792, but revoked by the Directory in 1795. Slavery was abolished in the French colonies by the National Convention in 1794, with Black people made equal to White people. However, slavery was re-established by Napoleon in 1802.

Many freedom seekers decided to emigrate to America, where the Constitution of the United States adopted in 1788, provided the world's first formal blueprint for a modern representative democracy.

Unlike the national assemblies of Europe, this government did not have to struggle with a monarch for political authority.

In the early nineteenth century, the United States extended suffrage to all white males (by removing property requirements). Never before had voting power belonged to such a large proportion of a national population. Thus, even though this level of suffrage hardly seems democratic today, the United States is often considered the world's first true democracy. (9)

Following this event, democracy gradually took hold across the West. The smoothest road lay in Britain, where Parliament continued to gain power at the expense of the monarch, and suffrage was finally extended. Throughout Continental Europe, democratization was a much more violent process, including many rebellions; notably, the year 1848 witnessed a wave of revolutionary struggles that gripped most Europe's nations.

Throughout the twentieth century, remaining barriers to suffrage (including discrimination based on gender and ethnicity) were finally removed in Western nations, such that universal suffrage was achieved. Today, it is estimated that some third of the world's nations use representative democracy and universal suffrage.

The Secret Ballot:

The notion of a secret ballot, where one is entitled to the privacy of their votes, is taken for granted by most today by virtue of the fact that it is simply considered the norm. However, this practice was highly controversial in the 19th century; it was widely argued that no man would want to keep his vote secret unless he was ashamed of it.

The motivation for the secret ballot is that was introduced the first time in Australia in 1856 was to avoid the buying and sales of votes, which was a highly common phenomenon, and to remove threats from i.e. employers, if the voter wanted to vote for a trade union friendly or leftist party.

As the mode of production changed during the industrial era and the economy shifted toward knowledge – the western world shifted toward representative democracy according to the liberal democratic model.

Everything done by society is an experiment on a grand scale, by analyzing which democracies have outlived the others, they have common principles – this are the principles of liberal democracy:

- Individual freedom: the right to personal property, life, freedom of feeling, believing, saying and writing whatever you want that is not discrimination or a secret of the state.

- A judiciary system with: the right to a fair trial with a lawyer, equality before the law, innocence until proven otherwise, no retroactive judgements, judgements that can be retried and a jury that is randomly elected from the people.

- Elections that are general, with one vote per person, in free, anonymous and recurring elections in a system of many parties, where the results are decided by a majority principle.

- Division of power: judging, executive and law-making as well as administrative independence from the others.

- A public information-principle, all public documents that are not secrets shall be accessible by the people.

- A constitution guarding the principles above.

Advantages of Representative Democracy:

· Sets limits to the Tyrants with law-making

· Different self-interests might get a chance of balancing each other

· Basically, it is still a hierarchic/authoritarian structure with some democratic feedback. You may call it elected dictatorship.

Disadvantages with Representative Democracy:

· It is cheaper to buy off a few politicians than an entire nation. It is a well-known fact that corruption is widespread in representative democracy

· Many people believe they have to be perfect to participate in politics and therefore avoid participating. Not everyone is willing to put up posters with His/her face all over the country, stating that you he the best and everyone shall vote on him?

· You don't use the full creativity and experience of the entire population while many talented people simply don't have time to do political campaigns and will not be included in major decisions.

· It is more about who will decide than what to decide.

· Politicians and Political Parties get dependent on campaign financing. As My acquaintance, senator Mike Gravel expressed it: In the US, your first obligation as a politician is to satisfy your campaign funders, secondly your party, and thirdly, the voters. Without support from the rich families in New York, your career is over in fifteen minutes...

· Politicians need to show that they have done something in order to get re-elected. The result is a vast number of unnecessary laws and regulations. This results in a draconic state apparatus with a suffocating and resource consuming bureaucracy. A Swiss book of law is much thinner than most other law books.

· High costs. Politicians tend to steadily increase their own wages and public spending, with high taxes as a consequence. Swiss taxes are famously low, without resulting in poverty and lack of social welfare and education.

· If the expert's rule, they are very likely to be selfish, and represent their own interests above the common interests. Just read the later chapter about corruption in the field of medicine if you don't believe this.

· Democracy without access to knowledge and education can become populism, a very ancient and actual problem, especially in developing countries.

· Hierarchic power structures within political organizations contributes to conformist and opportunistic thinking.

· No single individual is likely to agree on all points of a party program. Therefore, you must learn how to lie in public in order to become a politician and represent a political party.

· Politics and state activities is often decades behind the private industry because of the stiffness inherited in the bureaucratic political machine.

· Because of the above-mentioned reasons, participation in democratic movements and elections has steadily diminished in the last 30 years.

· All parties fight in order to get the sympathies of the middle voters. The choice will in the end be like choosing between Coca-Cola and Pepsi-Cola, but there is no way to get orange juice!

· Politicians seldom represent the average people, i.e., there are very few lonely immigrant mothers in most parliaments.

· Many voters fail to identify themselves with a particular political party or ideology. Would you accept to be forced to only have a choice between a few pre-packed bags of food, where all of them includes meat (especially if you happen to be a vegetarian)?

Direct Democracy in Switzerland:

Switzerland is a rare example of a country with instruments of direct democracy (at the levels of the municipalities, cantons, and federal state). Citizens have more power than in a representative democracy. At the federal level, citizens can propose changes to the constitution or ask for a referendum to be held on any law voted by the parliament.

Swiss citizens vote regularly on any kind of issue on every political level, such as financial approvals of a school house or the building of a new street, or the change of the policy regarding sexual work, or on constitutional changes, or on the foreign policy of Switzerland, four times a year. Between January 1995 and June 2005, Swiss citizens voted 31 times, on 103 federal questions besides many more cantonal and municipal questions. (13)

Switzerland has had tandem successes both socially and economically which are matched by only a few other nations, without having oil or major nature resources and has not been participating in any wars since the internal, religiously based Sonderband war in 1847, which led to the foundation of the Swiss Republic.

Direct Democracy also seems to give a very high rate of political stability.

The Swiss executive is one of the most stable governments worldwide. Since 1848, it has never been renewed entirely at the same time, providing a long-term continuity.

The Swiss government has been a coalition of the four major political parties since 1959, each party having a number of seats that roughly reflects its share of electorate and representation in the federal parliament.

In the US, about half of the member states have an Initiative and Referendum system similar to the Swiss for decision on local issues and state issues.

According DDB-Needham Advertising's Life Style Studies (11, 12), life satisfaction is measurably higher in states that allow initiatives than in those that do not. This holds even when controlling for a large range of other factors, including income, education, race, age, gender, employment status, personal health, marital status, and church attendance.

Satisfaction also increases with the cumulative use of initiatives over time. In other words, the more frequently a state has used initiatives to create its current policies, the happier people are.

States that use the initiative tend to have policies that help protect citizen prosperity, health, and security, all of which contribute to greater happiness.

This may be because citizens themselves use the initiative process to implement laws that directly aid them. Or it could be that legislators are more attentive to citizen well-being in states that have mechanisms for initiative, referendum, and recall. Either way, the net impact on both satisfaction and wellbeing is positive.

Perhaps more importantly, the study finds that lower- and middle-income people benefit most from initiatives. Simply put, the happiness of the rich and powerful in a state increases less relative to happiness boost that ordinary citizens receive.

One of the concrete results of the American referendums are the catalyzing systems for cleaning the exhaust fumes from car engines that now are obligatory on all kind of cars. This was the result of a popular vote in the state of California, and the Californian car market was so large, that the automobile industry was forced to adapt to the result of the Californian decision.

In Switzerland, voter turnout in parliamentary elections saw a continuous decline since the 1970s, down to an all-time low of 42.2% in 1995. In recent years however, voter participation has been slowly growing again and was at 48.5% in 2011. The average turnout for referendums was at 49.2% in 2011. Federal popular initiatives of little public appeal sometimes cause participation of less than 30% of the electorate, but controversial issues such as a proposed abolition of the Swiss army or a possible accession of Switzerland into the European Union have seen turnouts over 60%. (13)

It is interesting to note, that the participation rate is higher in the referendums, than in the parliamentary elections, who show a much lower participation rate than in most other western countries. The reason is that the Swiss don't care so much, who is in the government, because it does not matter so much, as they decide most the important issues in the referendums. many of them don't even know the name of their head of state. Do you know the name of the Swiss president?

The Swiss government also spends much less money on private jets, guards and wages for the politicians and the taxes are world famously low, without compromising with the social security.

One of the main arguments against the Swiss model is that the low voting turnout increases the risk for fanatic minorities, i.e. racist fractions or other subgroups of the population to get undue influence, because of the low voting percentage in some issues...

Investigations have also shown that a majority of the voters are middle aged men, and that many double working women don't have time to both take care of their work, the home and to educate themselves about the political issues and vote.

The Equations of Democracy:

If people where natural Saints, solving common problems would be much easier!

Humans are fundamentally egotistical, most often acting to maximize their own happiness – however in the social context a lot of people are egotistical, choosing short term gains over helping others for long term ones (if we all cooperated we would reach much further, as will be explained – however, if some people do not act for this, others will be less likely to as well, claiming "people are egotistical, so it does not matter what I do" – however, what you do matters, it can change the culture and the world).

If we were Christ like saints, who found it natural to love our neighbor as ourselves, we would probably not have the judiciary system or politics (as we know it at least). We would probably still have some democratic institutions to more easily synchronize our common concerns. Democracy is basically a way to solve conflicts between egoistical people and egoistic groups by using debate and voting instead of physical fights and war.

Now on to the democratic calculus and the dynamics of corruption.

The democratic calculus:

Egotistical people who focus on own profit short-term gains = E, as in Egoism.

There are positions of power in society = P, for Power.

$E + P \rightarrow$ Abuse of power.

As the short-sighted egoistic people are egoistic, the mathematical conclusion is that they will use this power for their own sake more than for the common good, otherwise they are not egoists, but altruists.

The ability to usurp selfish advantage by gaining power over others spontaneously creates a hierarchical organizational structure, where the most combative individuals with the sharpest elbows and biggest manipulation ability will end up in the top of the hierarchy. This fact is well verified and well documented in the bloody history of Man during the latest millennia.

R = Revolution. If a leader gets too brutal (or loses their material basis of power), they risk becoming a victim of mutiny or revolution. This risk increases the more people in your constituent group is brave, educated, communicative and have good ethics and self-esteem = B

This makes the leader's brutality usually to some extent limited, especially in small groups, where everyone knows each other. In large, hierarchical societies with different classes of people this relationship-based buffer is reduced, and situations such as concentration camps and mass slaughter may occur, such as with Hitler, Stalin, Kublai Khan, Mao Tse Tung, and the Emperor Leopold of Belgium in Congo.

In order to justify and preserve their power and dominate their subjects, the dictators have always employed virtually the same tricks, which we define as the oppressive force characteristics for O = Oppression:

1. Lies and Propaganda.

2. Censorship.

3. Personal Cult, with the portrait of the leader everywhere.

4. No Transparency, the important information is reserved for the few in power

5. Penalties and threats against dissidents.

6. Obedience gives you benefits, whether your conduct is ethical or not.

7. Creation of cohesion by creating conflicts against real or imaginary enemies and victimization of scapegoats.

8. Deprivation of citizens' self-esteem, courage, intellect, peer communication skills and educational attainment in order to keep everything under control.

9. Deliberate creation of filter-bubbles and mass hysteria.

10. Discouragement of independent thinking and personal initiatives.

You can quite easily use the above list to evaluate whether an organization or a company is good for you or not. Our advice is, if you are in an organization, with the leader's portraits on all the walls, opinion repression and propaganda, punishment of dissidents, where individual initiative and independent thinking is discouraged: Leave as fast as possible!

What we need to do to get a better society is simply to reverse the process and create a revolution against the tyranny by raising our level of Consciousness and Organize ourselves democratically:

$C + O = R$

C = Consciousness / Courage /Critical thinking.

In order to increase C, you just reverse O

[Dictatorial vs democratic properties below...]

1. Lies and Propaganda vs Truth and Honesty

2. Censorship vs Freedom of Speech and Independent Media

3. Personal Cult vs Egalitarity

4. No Transparency vs Transparency

5. Harsh Penalties and threats vs Minimum use of Penalties and threats

6. Obedience vs Freedom

7. Enemies and Scapegoats vs Tolerance against foreigners and minorities, privation of self-esteem, courage, encouragement of self esteem

9. Filter-bubbles and mass hysteria vs Critical Thinking

10. Discouragement personal initiatives vs Encouragement of Personal Initiatives

The revolutions have a tendency to not change very much, because society will often re-organize itself hierarchically again after the implementation of the revolution, i.e. Stalin and Lenin in the Soviet Union and Ayatollah Khomeini in Iran.

R + O = abuse of power.

In order to bring about Lasting change, one must therefore also carry out a democratic development = D. So, R + D = Lasting change for the better, therefore C + D = S, Successful Society = S.

C is raised for a bigger group in society as the material basis of society shifts its economy to a knowledge-basis, which also brings upon D.

Democracy works better with well-trained, brave and critical thinking people, while a fully functioning democracy increases the opportunity for free thinking, good education and courage.

Many investigations indicate that one of the key factors for prosperity, peace, health, good environment and quality of life and human development is the degree of democracy.

If you for example compare the list of the "happiest" countries with the human freedom index, which is a list based on human rights and democracy, you will find almost a linear relationship between degree of happiness and degree of democratic participation (11,12). The exception might be some countries with exceptional natural resources like Saudi Arabia and Kuwait.

Switzerland is the world's most democratic country and is at the top on all these parameters. Switzerland has, in addition to a democratically elected parliament also a tradition with many referendums and a well-developed local democracy, where decisions are made at the most local level possible. This will be elaborated more later in this chapter(13).

There are individuals in most societies with narcissistic and anti-social personality traits that have a pathological urge to attain power. These people will always look for power positions, no matter what the positions are called. In some societies they appear as politicians, in other as priests and in other as businessmen and lawyers. Certainly, a huge proportion ends up as medical doctors, as being an MD is still associated with prestige and power in many societies.

There is only one way to minimize their detrimental and dangerous influence on society, and that is to distribute the power as much as possible = Democracy.

The American author James Surowiecki addressed this issue in his book "The Wisdom of Crowds: Why the Many Are Smarter Than the Few and How Collective Wisdom Shapes Business, Economies, Societies and Nations, first published in 2004 (14). He postulates with the help of a large variety of practical examples and scientific experiments that informed crowds almost always performs better than any single member of the group even if certain individuals possess much more knowledge and experience than the average group members.

The opening anecdote relates Francis Galton's surprise that the crowd at a county fare accurately guessed the weight of an ox when their individual guesses were averaged. Surowiecki breaks down the advantages he sees in disorganized decisions into three main types, which he classifies as:

1. Cognition: Market judgment, which he argues can be much faster, more reliable, and less subject to political forces than the deliberations of experts, or expert committees

2. Coordination: Coordination of behavior includes optimizing the utilization of a popular bar and not colliding in moving traffic flows.

3. Cooperation. How groups of people can form networks of trust without a central system controlling their behavior or directly enforcing their compliance.

What makes a crowd wise:

Not all crowds (groups) are wise. Consider, for example, mobs or crazed investors in a stock market bubble or a crowd of Nazis burning synagogues and killing Jews. According to Surowiecki, these key criteria separate wise crowds from irrational ones:

1. Diversity of opinion: Each person should have private information even if it's just an eccentric interpretation of the known facts.

2. Independence: People's opinions aren't determined by the opinions of those around them.

3. Decentralization: Decisions become better, if people are able to specialize and draw on local knowledge.

4. Aggregation: Some mechanism must exist for turning private judgments into a collective decision.

5. Filter-bubbles: Surowiecki studies situations in which the crowd produces very bad judgment, and argues that in these types of situations their cognition or cooperation failed because (in one way or another) the members of the crowd were too conscious of the opinions of others and began to emulate each other and conform rather than think differently. Examples of such bubbles in the field of medicine is the case of puerperal fever (or childbed fever), which was one of the most common causes of early death in the 18th-19th century hospitals, with a mortality rate at 10%-35%. 1790, the Scottish surgeon James Gordon published a paper showing that the incidence of puerperal fever could be drastically cut by use of hand washing standards in obstetrical clinics. This was confirmed independently in 1847 by the Hungarian physician Ignatio Semmelweis. Despite Semmelweis publications by 1861 of statistical/clinical trials where hand-washing reduced mortality below 1%, Semmelweis' practice only earned widespread acceptance years after his death, when Louis Pasteur confirmed the germ theory in the 1890's. With a more unprejudiced and alert medical system, millions of premature mother deaths and family tragedies could have been prevented.

The solution to the world's problems is thus quite simple:

1. Improve democracy, both globally and locally.

2. Strengthen people's individuality, knowledge, critical thinking, education, self-esteem, communication, unity and courage and make sure everyone has access to unbiased information.

The more you strengthen number one, the more you will also strengthen number two and vice versa.

A positive spiral has been created!

Today, we are moving toward more authoritarian regimes, the answer lies in democracy and the information age – but first we need to understand the democratic deficit and corruption more analytically to construct the future bottom-up

References chapter 7:

1. Human Values and Beliefs A Cross-cultural Sourcebook av Miguel E Basanez, Ronald L Inglehart ISBN 9780472108336

2. The Muqaddimah An Introduction to History - Abridged Edition, Ibn Khaldun, N J Dawood, ISBN 9780691166285

3. The Medium is the Message An Inventory of Effects John Berger, Marshall McLuhan, Susan Sontag, Bruno Munari, ISBN 9780141035826

4. https://en.wikipedia.org/wiki/History_of_democracy

5. http://www.historyworld.net/wrldhis/PlainTextHistories.asp?ParagraphID=chy#ixzz4Ut7LBbgu

6. http://www.ancient.eu/Athenian_Democracy/

7. http://www.history.com/topics/ancient-history/ancient-greece-democracy

8. https://en.wikipedia.org/wiki/Martin_Luther 05.01.2017

9. http://www.essential-humanities.net/history-supplementary/democracy/

10. https://en.wikipedia.org/wiki/Direct_democracy

11. http://theconversation.com/direct-democracy-may-be-key-to-a-happier-american-democracy-52417

12. https://en.wikipedia.org/wiki/DDB_Needham_Life_Style_Surveys

13. https://en.wikipedia.org/wiki/Voting_in_Switzerland

14. "The Wisdom of Crowds: Why the Many Are Smarter Than the Few and How Collective Wisdom Shapes Business, Economies, Societies and Nations, ISBN-10: 0385721706

Illustrations chapter 7

1. https://www.needpix.com/photo/download/1509869/temple-palas-athens-parthenon-ancientgreece-greekgods-vintage-parthenon-in-athens-free-pictures
2. https://commons.wikimedia.org/wiki/File:Landsgemeinde_Glarus,_2009.jpg

Chapter 8: Liquid Democracy and Demosocracy.

The word liquid refers to liquid substance, like water. In water, the surface is always flat, and cannot become a pyramid. All the molecules can freely move around and communicate with each other, and information can spread freely in the shape of waves. Recent research has also shown that water can have memory and carry information, like in the experiments by the Nobel-Prize winner Luc Montagnier, who managed to transfer the energy pattern of a DNA molecule after diluting it to 10 hundred times until there were no molecules left in the water, transfer the energy pattern of the water over the internet from Paris to Rome and recreate it in Rome by exposing water and the building molecules of DNA for the frequencies from the water in Paris(1). Water is a magical substance, and the base for organic life on our Planet.

I am a little bit hesitant to use the word liquid in this book, as this word also has some negative and inappropriate associations connected. Liquid is associated with instability, and liquid as something you can drink in a bar. The word liquid Democracy was not invented by me. Before the name Liquid Democracy was proposed, I called my system Interactive Representative Direct democracy (IRD).

After many years of thinking on the subject, we now propose the word Demosocracy as a complement to the voting system Liquid Democracy, From Demos, which means free citizens, Sapiens which means wisdom and Kratia which means rule. By combining the experience of the people with the knowledge of the experts the outcome will be wise government. The term liquid democracy refers to a voting system, while the term *Demosocracy* to a new societal system based on liquid democracy and Demosocratic Consciousness.

How I came up with the idea of Demosocracy:

I was a kind of wonder child in philosophy and started having public lectures in advanced philosophy at the age of 17 and toured around Scandinavia as a very popular lecturer for couple for of years, besides studying music and medicine. In 1981, I got involved in the Green Party of

Sweden, and ended up on the election list for the parliament and became deputy member of the Council of Trustees, the party's highest decision-making body.

After a while he began to notice, that politicians do not have free rein. I remember that one of my ideas was to let government declare that Sweden was should give their whole defense budget to the UN if the UN promised to ensure Sweden's national security. If everyone did this, there would be peace on earth. For him, peace, democracy and international cooperation were the most important issues. I therefore had big problems arguing for Sweden not joining the European Union, which was the Green Party partisan line. This was also true of many other political issues that were close to my heart. In the end I decided to leave conventional politics. I was simply too bad at lying in public and had difficulties identifying with the "us and them thinking" that dominates party politics in representative democracy.

In the autumn 1992, I walked past a poster in Stockholm who advertised a new party called the Telephone Party. The message was that everyone could be able to participate in politics and political polls via a telephone keypad, according to the Swiss model. This party promised that if it got mandate in a political assembly, it would organize referendums in all the political issues and the party would commit to let the result of the telephone polls decide how they would vote. That is, a political party, which is totally controlled by its members. I thought it was an exciting idea, and directly contacted founder, Peter Ahlm, who also was the founder of the groundbreaking ad magazine, the Yellow Newspaper in Sweden.

His only argument against my system was that it could be difficult for everyone to get acquainted with all the issues and thus vote in a conscious way, which could lead to either a lot of unenlightened votes, or low voting turnouts. Experience shows that not even professional politicians have time to familiarize themselves with all the political issues in their own political assembly, much less in both the National, County and Municipal assemblies simultaneously. As a result of the low turnout in the referendums, there was a risk that extremist groups and unrepresentative minority formations could get an undue influence.

His proposed solution was that everyone should have the possibility to choose a representative or advisor who could vote for them in all matters in which they did not have enough time, knowledge or interest to participate actively, while they always could vote directly themselves when they wanted do it. The direct vote would always take precedence over the representative's voice. This voting system was later called Liquid democracy.

Delegated Voting

The advisor rates ideas and votes for the participant from now on = 2 possible outcomes

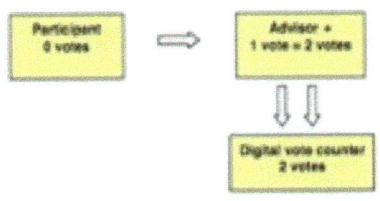

Delegated Voting

Participant's Vote **Always** Takes Precedence Over advisor's Vote.

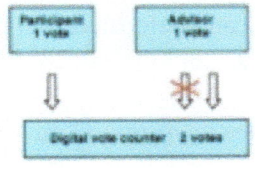

BUT...

Anyone can become an advisor, and representatives can be both individuals, organizations and political parties. You can change representative at any time, and you can have different representatives in various disciplines such as a qualified economist in economics and environmental scientist in environmental issues.

The Idea Greenhouse:

In Demosocracy, there will also be a system for creation and deliberation of political proposals called the idea greenhouse, where everyone can be able to suggest improvements of their society. These suggestions will then be reviewed and sorted by a review commission whose task it is to make the material manageable for the public, partly by sorting all the ideas under the correct headings, removing ideas which are already proposed and remove less serious suggestions or ideas contrary the constitution, for example, racist or discriminatory proposals. The work of the review commission will be totally open and transparent and everyone who is interested will be welcome to take part in that work, after a short introductory education on how it works.

The Idea Waste Basket:

To insure against corruption in the review commission all the rejected ideas would go to "the idea waste basket", where they would be publicly accessible to all participants. If many participants disagree that an idea should have been rejected idea, it can become re-approved.

All ideas can be debated with pro- and con arguments that in turn could be voted upon, and then sorted by popularity. In the end, each new proposal would be presented with weighted arguments for and against, and with how much votes the proposal received from the voters. The proposals that reach a certain level of popularity level predetermined by the participants will become official proposals and be investigated and implemented if they get a final approval from the participants.

One can also use the above-mentioned Idea generating system to resolve political problems.

In the early 2000s, the State of California had a major energy crisis, both from trouble with smog and environmental pollution and from high energy prices / availability. My company Vivarto AB then created an Internet debate with the question "How can we solve California's energy problems." Everyone could submit proposals, vote and debate on the proposals according to the principles above.

The participants almost unanimously concluded that the smartest thing would be to invest into solar power plants in the desert and let the cars be powered by electricity or fuel cells. Now, 15 years later, it seems that this is actually going to happen !!! In 2011 the US government created a website called www.challenge.org, who works in a similar way, with one difference, the final decision is with the government officials and not with the participants.

Demosocracy is inspired by the human brain.

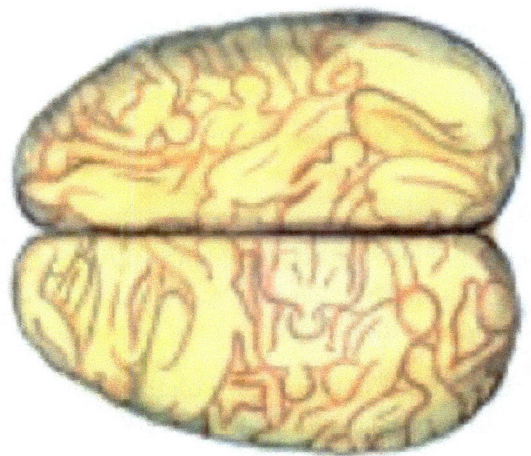

(This picture above by Arnstein Myggland is a brain made up by people, symbolizing collective Intelligence.)

In order for us to function as human beings, it is important to have a balance between habits and automatic behaviors and the ability to be flexible and learn new things, otherwise we cannot survive. An example of this is a syndrome called Ondine's syndrome.

Ondine was a nymph, a water goddess in a French folk tale written by Friedrich de la Motte Fouqué.

She was breathtakingly beautiful and possessed of a streak of independence, truly what we call a 'free spirit'.

Like all nymphs and mermaids, she was leery of men. If a nymph ever falls in love with a man and bears his child, she will begin to age like a mortal woman, losing her eternal youthfulness and everlasting life.

Nonetheless, when Ondine saw the handsome young Palemon she was smitten and began to watch for him on his daily walks. When Palemon noticed her, he was taken by her incredible beauty and came back frequently to try to get a glimpse of her again.

Eventually they talked and fell in love. He broke his engagement with the young noblewoman Berta and, in time, convinced Ondine to marry him. When they exchanged their wedding oaths, Palemon vowed that "My every waking breath shall be my pledge of love and faithfulness to you." But it was not to be.

The following year Ondine gave birth to their son. From that moment on, her beauty began to fade, her body suddenly susceptible to the effects of age. As her youthful attractiveness gave way to a more mature beauty, Palemon's eye began to wander to the younger women he met at court.

One fateful day Ondine was out walking on their estate when she heard the sound of Palamon's familiar snoring. Planning to take him back home so he could finish his nap, the amused Ondine entered the stables to wake him.

The scene she encountered filled her with great sorrow. Discarded garments littered the floor and her beloved Palemon lay sleeping in the haystack, his arms wrapped around his former fiancé Berta. Having sacrificed her immortality for this man, she was filled with anger and regret.

Kicking her sleeping husband, she woke him and uttered her curse. "You pledged faithfulness to me with your every waking breath and I accepted that pledge. So be it. For as long as you are awake, you shall breathe. But should you ever fall into sleep, that breath will desert you."

Ondine still retained some of her magic . . . enough to make the curse come true. And so it was. Palemon would never sleep again(13).

When you have the Ondine's syndrome, you stop breathing when you feel asleep, and you will die unless you connect yourself to a respirator before falling asleep. In other words, all of us are totally dependent on automated functions that works all the time without we needing to give them attention, otherwise we cannot function. These tasks can be immensely complicated and can take long time to learn, but without them becoming automated, our mind would become overloaded and not be able to perform all the essential functions in the body. The automated part of our consciousness corresponds to the delegated voting in Demosocracy. On the other hand, it is important to also have the ability to be mentally active and focus on new tasks and learning, otherwise we would be a robot that cannot learn, and not a human being. This part corresponds to the direct participation in Demosocracy.

The Direct Party:

Peter Ahlm was not interested in the idea of liquid democracy, or interactive representative direct democracy as it was called by then, so I decided to launch a new political party, The Direct Party, which was formed in 1993. also had the intention of binding their mandate to the results of the referendums via touchtone phone / Internet (Internet was almost unknown by then), but with the addition of an automatically programmed representative system.

The Direct Party achieved around 300 members, but did not assess that this was enough to attend the election in 1994. It received some attention in the media and I participated in quite a few newspaper, radio and TV interviews, including a television program called "Can we trust our politicians" with, among others former Prime Minister of Sweden, Carl Bildt and the leading opposition politician Mona Sahlin.

From 1985 - 1994, I had mainly made my living me as a musician traveling playing own arrangements of classical masterpieces on synthesizers, as well as own compositions with symphonic synthesizer music. This had gone incredibly well for many years, especially since I also started selling self-produced CDs in conjunction with the performances. After 1992, my music business went down, probably because of more and more advertising-based cable TV channels, free newspapers and the development of Internet.

This led me to resume my old career as a medical doctor. Since I did not had so much experience and had not been active as a physician in 8 years, I had to take the jobs that were offered, and that was not in Sweden, but in Norway. When I moved, I had, of course, difficulties simultaneously being a party leader in Sweden, and when he disappeared, so did the Direct Party. I had unfortunately not been able to inspire enough people that could carry on the party independently of him, without its founder and driving force.

Vivarto Inc.

I continued to work in psychiatry, and later returned to Sweden where I began working on a doctoral dissertation together with Professor Ulf Malm from the Sahlgrenska University Hospital in Gothenburg about the social network's importance for psychotic illnesses.

I also wrote an international bestseller about depression treatment with the herbal medicine St John's Wort 1997 together with the American authors Peter McWilliams and Harold Bloomfield. In 1999 I was on the way to my work at the psychiatric clinic in Handen, south of Stockholm. It was a beautiful winter day with a lot of ice on the roads. I was late, and decided to run the slippery shortcut through the forest from the commuter train station to my workplace in order to spare time, and IIIIIHHH. KaDonk!!! I laid down, in the middle of the forest with a severely broken ankle. Luckily, I had a cell phone and could call for an ambulance. It hurt like hell, and the paramedics had to use half a pharmacy to ease my pain (He was 199 cm tall and weighted 120 kg).

I was operated immediately and had to spend six weeks with a plaster afterwards.

During these six weeks, I had planned to take a week's winter holiday to go skiing in the Alps together with my future wife, Dina. This was of course impossible with a plaster on the foot, so I had to cancel the trip, with the result that the I suddenly had a week off. I then got a tip o that I could work as a so-called leasing doctor and get paid quite a lot per invoice.

At the same time, I had more and more noted how the many savings and the often-incompetent management had resulted in a more and more declining quality of work, where I worked and also in many other working places...

Politicians appointed managers who were more interested in budgeting than human beings, with the result that all qualified employees became sick or resigned, after which a paralyzing mixture of fear and incompetence started to spread in the institution.

I then got the idea that this problem most likely could be solved if we instead of working with hierarchical organizational models used cooperative networks supported by Liquid Democracy.

This meant that I decided to quit psychiatry and started working as leasing doctor, and invest the surplus from leasing doctor activities in the development of a software for Liquid Democracy, NetConference Plus through the company, Vivarto AB.

This time, the strategy wasn't to create a new political party, but as a company influence that could the parties, organizations and companies to start using new, more democratic organizational models.

The IT operations of Vivarto started in 1999. using the surplus from the medical activities to fund software development using cheap programmers from ex-Yugoslavia.

Vivarto's first customer was the multi-media education at the University of Stockholm, which used NetConference Plus to evaluate and discuss their course program. Later we got Haninge Youth Council, the trade union TCO, Umeå Student Union, Hals Municipality in Denmark, Camden and Southwalk City Councils in London and the youth union of the Swedish Liberal Party became customers. In cooperation with the American company Safevote, Vivarto carried out Sweden's first official Internet election for the student association at the university of Umeå in the Spring of 2001. This was a success, and in 2002 they were contracted to perform the biggest Internet election test in history so far in cooperation with the Swedish government and the biggest newspaper in Sweden's, Aftonbladet. We were supposed to let 300 000 high school students make a test vote on the Internet, which unfortunately partly failed because Safevote's servers had too poor capacity.

That was probably the main reason for the bankruptcy of Vivarto in 2004.

Vivarto also starred in a series of conferences and events together with the EU IT Commission, the Swedish government, The Canadian government, the Finish and English parliaments, Democracy Collaborative in Washington, and the National Democratic Institute in the United States. In autumn 2003, the undersigned was invited as an expert to the World Political Forum in Turin under the leadership of Mikhail Gorbachev, and was introduced as the "Benjamin Franklin of the Future World Democracy" before UN deputy Secretary General, Benon Sevan and 50 heads of state and former heads of state. In 2002 Netconference also was mention as "the world's most advanced democracy Software" by the National Democratic Institute in Washington, headed by the ex- foreign minister of the US, Madeleine Albright.

Vivarto has also held several high-level meetings with the United Nations and included the Invited to speak at Stanford and other universities in the US and other parts of the world.

In 2003 I also published the book "How to make a bunch of lazy and selfish people work together with the help of modern information technology", which, inter alia, Was very well received when it was presented at the World Social Forum in Bombay in 2004 (15).

Vivarto AB was unfortunately like many other IT -companies, amongst them our main competitor, Votia AB, bankrupt in 2004, primarily due to a server breakdown associated with the Young Election 2002, and the lack of investors who were willing to invest in new IT ideas after the big IT crash in 2001.

Demoex:

In 2002, me and the very dedicated teacher Per Norbäck together few students from Vallentuna, north of Stockholm founded the Demosocracy Party Demoex. It was built on the same idea as the Direct Party. They received a mandate in the city council and in 2003 became Parisa Molagoli, the representative of Demoex in the city council was chosen to be "the politicians of the year" in Vallentuna. They used Vivarto's software NetConference Plus until December 2004 after which it could no longer be supported due to the bankruptcy of Vivarto AB.

Demoex has been appreciated in Swedish media, and was chosen to be one of the 100 best websites in Sweden in 2003, before among others MSN!

Demoex managed to influence and change many decisions in the local parliament, in spite of the fact that they did have only one seat. Among else they managed to turn down a suggestion for increased salary to local politicians! In a scientific evaluation performed by Karin Ottesen, from Mitthögskolan, in Sundsvall, Sweden, she concluded that flexible representation by Delegated voting "probably serves its purpose, which is to Decrease the pressure laid upon the Participants and Increase the number of given votes in every certain voting "(17).

Later on the Demoex, Äkta Demokrati(Real Democracy) and Aktiv Demokrati(Active Democracy) has joined forces and created a joint party called Direktdemokraterna(http://direktdemokraterna.se/). They have developed a software called GOV(https://www.facebook.com/groups/gov.online.voting) Unfortunately, there have been many internal conflicts and problems managing the software in this group, which has led to a less exciting development. Other projects, like Syntropis Crowdpol believes in changing the system from outside instead of through a party.

Liquid Democracy Now:

In recent years, Liquid Democracy has received a boost and several books have been written on the subject (1-5), Google did develop a software which they tested at 15 000 employees (6) and more and more organizations and political parties have begun to use Demosocracy, or Liquid Democracy.

One of the persons I met in New York in 2001 together with Professor Benjamin Barber, who invited him to the meeting of the World Democratic

Council, was Beth Noveck, who later Became the director of President Obama's Open Government Initiative. She was obviously interested in some of my ideas and spoke about them on many occasions and mentioned them in her book, Wiki Democracy(9).

Pirate Parties in Germany, Italy, Austria, Norway, France and the Netherlands use Liquid Democracy with the open-source software Liquid Feedback, while members of the Belgian Pirate Party have developed Their own software called Get Opinionated.

In Spain the "Partido de Internet" developed its own software platform for voting, now an independent free-software and commercial project called Agora Voting.

In the Australian federal election, 2016, the Flux (political party) contested Senate seats in New South Wales, Victoria, Western Australia, South Australia and Tasmania on the platform of using Blockchain technology to enable a form of delegate democracy (though the site itself does not explicitly describe the model as either delegate or Liquid Democracy)(9).

In the US, a party has recently been started called US Direct Democratic party who are developing a software called igov. Direct(https://democracy.onl/us/)

At the 2013 general election the Italian Five Star Party was the most voted party for the Chamber of Deputies, but obtained just 109 deputies out of 630 due to an electoral system which favored parties running in coalition. In total, it is now the second biggest party in Italy with about 30% of the voters. In June 2016, Virginia Raggi, a 37-year old M5S candidate, was elected mayor of Rome with 67% of the votes. Her victory was complemented by the election of another movement candidate in Turin, 31-year-old Chiara Appendino, who overtook the previous mayor and founder of the Democratic Party(8). In the 2018 general election, the M5S became the largest individual party in the Italian Parliament and entered government.

The Italian five-star movement proposes Liquid Democracy and has been using many different direct democracy platforms, including Aeresis and

Liquid Feedback. One of the problems that has been facing the 5SM after starting to govern is the massive tradition of corruption and mafia in Italy, which somehow demands you to be a tough fighter in order to resist it, which can be hard, when you have a very great variety of voters supporting you, from both left and right.

There are also still technical issues to solve, especially regarding education of users and user friendliness of the software's, security, verifiability and personal anonymity, but it seems pretty clear to me that the future of Democracy will be digital, no matter what we do or believe.

Advantages with Demosocracy:

· Bigger Selection of representatives/advisors, it is very likely that you can know them personally and that they will have the required knowledge and talents to represent you adequately.

· You can always vote yourself

· The one who decides when to take part directly or indirectly is you and no-one else.

· You can most likely find an entity or a person who you know personally to be a delegate for you when using delegated voting. This is the way our species have lived most of our time on planet earth, delegating voting or responsibility based on personal knowledge and trust within the tribe.

· Combines participation and expertise, you are not forced to choose between a corrupted expert or an unenlightened crowd anymore.

· The new possibilities of participation will probably lead to more politically mature and educated people.

· The expert advisors do not have to make a political career in order to be noticed, they can focus on solving problems, instead of wasting energy and money on political campaigns.

· Demosocracy utilizes the common creativity and knowledge of the entire population, in her book "Smart Citizens, Smarter State, the political advisor and cyber democracy expert Beth Noveck postulates that better utilization of the local expertise and the talents of people within society in order to solve common problems is one of the key challenges for a successful society(26). In the field of medicine, the government tends to rely on professors who has made a career within the corrupted system. In order to succeed with that you have to be obedient and value money and prestige more than truth and the health of your patients. Honest and intelligent experts will instead most likely lose their license and be maligned in media. With Demosocracy, people like me and other medical freedom fighters could have a chance to have influence.

· It can activate participants who cannot identify with one of the present political parties.

· You don't have to pretend to be perfect in order to participate in politics.

· Collective Intelligence gives more transparency, and less big power positions to fight about.

· It is much more expensive to bribe one million people than to bribe one politician, and harder not to get caught!

· More people will be able to view and investigate common decisions.

· Everyone will be represented equally.

· You do not have to be a political conformist in order to qualify as advisor.

· More co-operation and less fighting, Experiences from Swiss democracy clearly shows this phenomenon.

· The focus will be more on what to decide instead of who will decide.

· The process can be self-improving, with the possibility of writing proposals on how to improve the system as part of the project.

· Democracy is good at including externalities.

· Creates an ordered mass-discussion to find the grand-narrative which solves the problem in every single narrative.

· It avoids Arrow's impossibility-theorem as it can include ranking of options by Condorcet-choice.

Problems with Demosocracy:

· NO 1 Most people are brainwashed by school and society that there are no alternatives to the current system, that people are too egoistic to co-operate, etc. It will take lots of time to break this spell and maybe even many new generations.

· Many people do not have access to and knowledge about how to use computers and Internet.

· Many do not believe Demosocracy will work and do not want to spend time studying how to use the new democratic possibilities.

· It is hard and challenging to make a complex software system that is stable, have the necessary features and is user-friendly.

· The people in power seldom want to risk losing their present privileges by implementing change.

· People know what they have, but not what they will get. A general fear and resistance towards the unknown.

· In a situation, where you have to fight against mafia and corruption, i.e. trying to change the medical patent laws or be the mayor of Rome, it can be hard to be efficient and swift enough when you have to use time consuming e-democracy tools.

· It takes time to establish a new political culture

· Unless there is really something at stake, voter participation tends to be low.

United Individuals - A Proposal for a New Kind of World Governance

Below we will move forward an idea on how to use the best from Athenian Direct Democracy, Swiss Democracy Representative Democracy and Demosocracy in order to create a better world.

Many leading politicians and scientists agree upon the fact that we need to strengthen global democracy in order to combat problems like the greenhouse effect, wars, terrorism, global epidemics and starvation. Calculations has shown, that if we could use only 1% of the world income in a synchronized an efficient manner for these purposes, many of these problems could be solved.

The United Nations has tried to achieve many of the above-mentioned goals, but has only limited success so far. One of the main reasons might be that nations hesitate to give up some of their national sovereignty for common purposes. Another that the member nations have a non-optimal, democratic decision-making structure, with too many middle-men between the citizens and the decision-makers and a security council with very little democratic input.

UN also have very small economic and military power compared to the big nations like China, India Russia and the US.

Global Democracy - An uncharted territory!

As there is presently no effective and democratically controlled world government and world law, you can say that the Global democracy domain is like an uncharted territory!

This means, that we just like the pilgrims on the ship Mayflower, now have the opportunity to sit down and make new, better rules for how to organize the new, unknown continent. No-one can stop us from doing this, if we just decide to do it! No revolution is needed!!

If the financial markets can, we can also do it!

The financial markets have already organized and decentralized themselves by using the resources of the Internet. This has resulted to an increase in power in favor of the market forces. Now it is time for the citizens of our Planet to also get organized in order to civilize and regulate these powers.

Market economy can also be seen as decentralized direct democratic system, where every dollar you spend on a product can be seen as a vote to increase the production of that entity. The problem with market economy is the tendency for all the votes to end up in a few rich hands.

How to start?

One of the main problems with organizing a global democracy over the internet is that most people do not have interest, access or education enough to take part in such an experiment. To organize a world-wide Demosocracy System over the Internet can to many people seem like a Utopian vision and would most likely strongly favor the western well-educated countries, where the Internet access and literacy is much higher. In many countries like China, the Internet is also under censorship, which is a major problem for the development of an International Cyber Democracy.
If you want to construct a World Parliament using traditional Elections and election campaigns, this will be very hard because:

· Many dictatorship countries will most likely not allow free elections

· Huge costs for arranging elections and election campaigns

A representative world parliament will also face all the classical problems of representative democracy mentioned above with corruption, lobbyism, dependence on campaign financing etc.

<u>Chamber 1: A Randomly Assigned World Parliament</u>

One way to solve this problem to construct a World Parliament, where people from all countries and parts of the world are randomly selected to become World Parliamentarians, according to the ancient Greek model. The parliamentarians will get a salary, secretaries and education if needed.

By using such a system, not only the rich and famous but also experiences from the uneducated slums and from poor people in poor countries will be represented, which in our opinion is extremely essential. The parliament should have a physical location with physical facilities where the parliamentarians can meet. We suggest one parliamentarian for each 10 millions of world population. This body can serve as a one of the chambers of the world parliament that will truly represent the people's interests, and not be diverted by the power elite.

It is of course very important to adopt strict rules against lobbyism corruption for the parliament members.

Chamber 2: An Electronic World Parliament based on Demosocracy

The problem with randomly selected world parliament is that this will leave 99.99999% of the population with very little influence on world politics, leaving a majority of the world population passive and without power, thus not utilizing the creative power of the entire population.

Therefore, we should besides the randomly selected world parliament also make an electronic word parliament based on Demosocracy, where all world citizens will be invited to participate, with the possibility to make proposals, vote on and discuss issues that needs to be solved on world level.

The delegated voting system will help overcoming the digital divide issue, as i.e. an entire village can be represented by a common advisor who has computer access.

How to make Decisions

Our suggestion is that proposals for new laws and international policies must be approved by both chambers of the world parliament in order to be implemented. In case of conflicts between the two chambers, the issue has to be readdressed and reformulated.

World Government

The World parliament will appoint persons for different positions in the executive branch of the world parliament, with the task to implementing the decisions made by the parliament. To make sure that there will only be qualified and mentally fit people in positions of administration, these positions can be elected, with every participator having to send in his CV. They also have to perform psychological profiles and personality tests in order to sort out persons with a master/slave mentality and psychopathic narcissistic traits.

World Court

We suggest that we in the world court use the old Athenian system, where the verdict in each case can be voted upon by the two chambers in the world parliament. By using Demosocracy and delegated, no-one will be exhausted with too many decisions.

Subsidiarity

It is of course very important, that the new world parliament and world government only will deal with issues that cannot be solved at regional, local or personal level. All decisions should be made on the lowest possible subsidiary level, preferably on the personal level. You can say this is one of the definitions of freedom: The only reason for making common decisions is when a certain issue might interfere with the individual freedom of others. Then we need to use the democratic tools to find a wise compromise that balances all the individual interests optimally.

Financing of the World Parliament

In the beginning, we might need funding from philanthropists, funds and crowd funding.

When the World Parliament gets real power, we suggest one of the first issues should be to claim all-natural resources like oil, minerals and gas as property of the world. Market economy is good for buying and selling things and services you have produced. Natural resources have not been produced, but are gifts from nature, that also needs to be carefully nursed.

Just owning some land above an oil well should not give you trillions of dollars for nothing and does not contribute to society at all. If all the money now being paid because a private person, a nation or a company happens to sit on some kind of natural resource would be entitled the entire humanity, this would be enough to eradicate most diseases, illiteracy and poverty from the planet.

The final battle

We cannot expect the current corrupted world leaders, media, pharmaceutical companies, war industry producers, banks and army leaders to support a worldwide direct democracy. I just read an article in the Swedish liberal newspaper about Beppe Grillo and the five-star movement, where they called him populist and an "almighty establishment critic", comparing him to Berlusconi, not mentioning a word about the direct democratic organization of the party(10).

Almost no-one we know, even people who are working for the direct democratic party in Sweden did not know that Italy´s biggest party according to opinion polls in January 2017 is proposing Liquid Democracy and Direct Democracy.

All truth passes through four stages, according to J.B.S. Haldane. First, it is silenced and not noticed, secondly it is ridiculed and violently opposed. Third, it is trivialized. Fourth, it is accepted as being self-evident, the former opponents might claim it was their idea from the very beginning, and they now try to find out how they can manipulate in order fit it for their own purposes.

Demosocracy is mainly in stage 1 currently, but we can expect all the other stages to come as soon as it will break the publicity barrier. We can expect lots of lies and disinformation in media, legal threats and direct violence and threats about violence, everything that we already did mention in the chapter about how the medical industry rules the health sector.

This battle will most likely be the final real battle on our planet. Without corruption, dictatorship, unregulated capitalism and sovereign nations we will very likely live peacefully forever after.

Summary: Democracy:

· Our natural state in the majority of the last millions of years have been to live in a tribe where there was a combination of hierarchy, with the chief in charge, and direct democracy, where everyone could influence issues and decisions, somehow in proportion to their position in the hierarchy.

· With the invention of agriculture and private property, conflicts over ownership and land increased, leading to the development of greater social units organized into classes, like nobility, priests, soldiers and peasants, craftsmen and slaves. This gave rise to authoritarian, hierarchic power structures.

· A big army often beats a small army. The cultures who could organize themselves better into big entities and mobilize many soldiers survived, and conquered and enslaved the more peaceful cultures.

· In ancient Greece, the Philosophers Solon and Cleisthenes proposed a revolutionary new organization model called direct democracy. It led to one of the most important cultural, philosophic and scientific periods in modern history. One interesting anti-corruption experiment was to appoint eligible candidates to power positions by lottery and not by election.

· Democracy and Culture/Freedom/Education goes hand in hand. More Democracy gives more culture, and vice versa. Both are equally important to create a good society.

· It is of utmost importance to avoid so called rational bubbles, or mass hysteria if you want a well-functioning democracy. Individual thinking and scientific deduction methods must be important subjects in education.

· There is almost a linear relationship between the amount of democratic participation and quality of life in different societies.

· The ancient Rome was partly inspired by the Athenian democracy, although it was too big to make place for all the free citizens to fit into a square. Therefore representative democracy was invented. The development of the printing press, the universities with publication of scientific papers and free access to knowledge and increasing literacy created the ground for the development of free thinking and representative democracy, that succeeded to become the dominant political system in the western world in the 20th century.

· The exception is Switzerland, who with success has developed a more direct democratic system.

· The development of telecommunications, better and cheaper travelling and the Internet has united the world physically, but not yet politically. This has left a power vacuum that has been filled by multinational corporations, with the result that a few wealthy owner families have become unofficial world dictators, or oligarchs.

· Representative democracy is very vulnerable to corruption through dependence on campaigning funds, lobbyism and bribery. It also leads to unnecessary bureaucracy and taxes.

· Lack of democratically controlled international legislation has led the pharmaceutical/medical business to become one of the most corrupted entities in world history, causing millions of unnecessary deaths every year, partly because of side effects of often unnecessary medicines, partly because of suppression of non-patentable treatments.

· As there currently is no well-functioning world government and world law, global democracy is liked an uncharted territory. No one can actually stop us if we just organize ourselves. No revolution is needed, although we cannot expect the current system to fall without a fight.

· The development of Internet has enabled a new political system to be developed called Demosocracy, which combines the best from representative and direct democracy and has the probable possibility to reduce corruption and bureaucracy and increase the use of "the wisdom of the crowd".

· One way to obtain a functioning world democracy would be to combine the old Athenian principle to elect world parliament members by random lottery with another parliament chamber governed by a worldwide Demosocracy system, where everyone can participate.

References chapter 8:

1.http://library.uniteddiversity.coop/Decision_Making_and_Democracy/Democracy2.1.pdf

2. Anders Lönnfält, Joakim Sigvald, Flytande demokrati (2014) ISBN 9789198107517

3. http://demoex.se/files/Ottesensuppsats.pdf

4. https://www.amazon.com/The-Little-Horse-Athens-ebook/dp/B00A414T9I

5: Jan Behrens, Axel Kistner, Andreas Nitsche, Björn Swierczek The Principles of LiquidFeedback ISBN 978-3-00-044795-2

6. http://www.tdcommons.org/cgi/viewcontent.cgi?article=1092&context=dpubs_series

7. https://www.brookings.edu/book/wiki-government/

8. https://en.wikipedia.org/wiki/Delegative_democracy

9. http://thegovlab.org/democratizing-policymaking-online-liquid-feedback/

10. http://www.occupy.com/article/5-star-rise-italys-first-crowd-sourced-party-delivers-direct-democracy-action#sthash.3SeQYTwT.dpuf

11. De Rosa. R "The Five Stars Movement in the Italian Political Scenario A Case for Cybercratic Centralism:" https://www.researchgate.net/publication/303898637

Chapter 9: Demosocratic Economy.

The Demosocratic Co-operative:

As we read above, the world of today is dominated by multi-national companies and banks, and these companies, in turn, are almost organized according to the hierarchical/authoritarian model, thus enforcing the meme of slavery.

A few rich investors, banks and hedge funds basically control the entire political and economic system.

Very few have questioned the capitalistic model of enterprise, which is the backbone in the current economy.

Me, and also most other people I know don't like to be employed, neither to be bosses or to work alone.

My solution is the liquid co-operative, where all major decision in the co-operative will be made by using the principles of Demosocracy. Every participant can propose what he think needs to be done. The other members can in the first stage propose improvements and amendments to his proposal. After the proposal has been fixed, it can be debated upon and investigated more thoroughly, i.e. how much resources that need to be allocated in order to perform the proposal and who will be capable of executing it.

Then the co-workers put a price tag on the mission and decide if it will be done and who will do it. In the Demosocratic co-operative, all internal payments will be done by an intrinsic payment system, meaning that the co-operative cannot go bankrupt because of salary debts.

Each member can then exchange his internal money to dollars, euro or any other fiat currency depending on how much fiat currency is available in the co-operative if needed.

You only get paid for well-performed work, and no-one is exploiting or using anyone else. The cost for supervision, bureaucracy, and control will also be minimal. They will also use the full scope of creativity of all the co-workers and have less stress, boredom, sick leave from work and other slavery-related problems.

We believe that if we can make these kinds of co-operative structures work, they can, in the long run, compete very efficiently with the capitalistic companies and make the current business system obsolete by beating capitalism on the market place, on its own home ground.

The patent-system:

The patent-system is a horrible system today which is a great marginal cost for society. Marianne Mazzucato showed in her book "The entrepreneurial state" that the state is the greatest entrepreneur in the western society today, creating most ideas – companies patent the states ideas, how? It has to do with the academy, in universities a lot of cooperation happens (even if it is elitist) and the results are patented by companies who give the workers low-wages and bad working-spaces etc.... This is a cost in money and happiness for the people. David Noble and Noam Chomsky have also criticized the patent system, it makes sure so that the companies' parasites on the science-community and that the patent lawyers get a lot of money which gives rise to high administrative costs.

Stiglitz price-proposal: you get a price instead of a patent, Global Intellectual Property's center criticized this, claiming this idea is good for ideas and not material things – however, today, material things are not difficult to make in the western world and the ideas are in focus. Prizes is the way to go, the patent system is an outdated pathological hierarchy.

How to create a new monetary-system:

The monetary system needs to be changed, the effects of creating money from thin air by private banks giving out loans changes inflation in a way that is not beneficial for the people. It is true that inflation can work in Keynesian economic policy to lower macro-instabilities – helicopter-money can be put into the poor areas of society to lower the costs there, it is a much better stability-method than Quantitative Easing which only helps the rich get richer (a sort of socialism for the rich - In his book "Superclass"(1) David Rothkopf states that "The top 100 financial institutions in the world manage nearly $43 trillion, or about one-third of the world's global financial assets.

Of ten thousand hedge funds worldwide, the top one hundred, just over 1 percent, control an estimated 60 percent of the industry's $2 trillion in assets. One investor, Fidelity, with nearly $2 trillion

in assets, owns 10 percent or more of one hundred of America's largest companies.).

This enormous increase of wealth in the hands of a few super-rich financial families is an unavoidable consequence of the current, totally illogical and corrupted "Fractional Reserve Banking" system, where the banks create money by giving out loans from thin air. As these loans are connected to a money lending interest, new money always has to be created in order to cover up for the surplus needed to be paid back to the bank as interest by the bank customer. This will unavoidably lead to an enormous accumulation of capital in the financial markets(inflation), and a lack of capital in the real economy(deflation), until the economy finally totally will collapse.

In order to create a real base for a currency, labor time is the ideal new "Gold Standard", as time is a universal unit, and equally available to us all.

I therefore suggest we instead make a time-based, interest free currency based on working hours, issued by a demosocratic government.

One average unqualified labor hour could be the standard unit, and very qualified workers can get more than one working hour per hour in payment, but there should be a limit to the number of working hours one can earn per hour and possess in order to inhibit unlimited capital accumulation.

The time-base makes sure that the value of production equals the value of the money and consumption such that no instability is created.

Price Planning:

The whole people can take part in setting the prices, for cooperatives as well, by the principle of central-price planning. The central board can be the entire people and they will follow the following optimally according to Oskar Lange(2)

1. They will construct factor-evaluation tables for which they substitute the expected values of the factors.

2. The functions are then assumed as the managers of all operative production and are assumed to be entirely correct.

3. The result will indicate exactly which factors needs a change.

4. If there are changes necessary, the factor-evaluation tables get new substitutions for those factors of the new expected values.

This process is repeated.

(1.) can be based upon historical information.

The price planning leads to full employment and a small economic cycle.

Lange himself thought that the minor areas of production, like farming, should not have central price planning.

The only three information-pieces necessary to carry this out are:

1. A preference scale showing actions (an indicator giving the demand of each product).

2. The production-functions (the terms for which alternatives are offered, i.e. how much does the workers cost, the capital, etc...).

3. Knowledge about how many resources are usable totally.

This solves the problem of quantitative-changes instead of price-changes in capitalism, people do not need to lose their jobs.

Project Cybersyn used this during the 1970's (not with Demosocracy) and it was successful.

Participatory economy (parecon)(3) is also made a possibility, where consumers and producers decide together on quantity and quality, a negotiated coordination. Peer-reviewing should be obligatory anonymous –

idea debates should not affect or be affected by who the people are in the debate.

Bertrand Russell wrote: assume that a certain number of people are momentarily working with creating needles, they create as many as the world needs in, say, 8 hours per day. Someone creates a machine that can create twice as many needles – the world, however, does not need twice as many needles: needles are already cheap, so cheap that more would not be sold to a lower price. In a reasonable world, the people who worked with creating needles would start working 4 hours instead of 8, and everything else would be the same. But in the existing world, this is considered demoralizing. People still work for 8 hours, there is an over-production of needles, some companies fail, and half of the people who worked with creating needles loses their jobs. In the end, there is the same amount of spare-time as before, but half of the workers lost their jobs and have nothing to do, as the other still works as hard. In this way, the spare-time becomes a pathway to misery instead of happiness. Can you possibly imagine anything more retarded?

Soon, automated machines and robots will perform 90% of the work, it is just a matter of time until the whole transportation industry will be automated with self-driving cars, busses, and trucks, leaving millions of transportation workers unemployed. What can we do to make this change become a resource for humanity instead of a cause of misery and unemployment?

Elites in society have a huge concentration of power, and humans are unpredictable, therefore the future in the elitist/authoritarian society becomes unstable – let us make it stable and make the future great again.

References chapter 6:

1. Rothkopf, David (2008) Superclass: The Global Power Elite and the World They Are Making Farrar   ISBN-10: 9780374531614

2. Lange, O 1942 Economics of Socialism Journal of Political Economy 50(2):299-303Chapter 9

3.   https://en.wikipedia.org/wiki/Participatory_economics

Illustration: https://pixabay.com/sv/photos/bank-pengar-finans-aktier-spara-2907728/

Chapter 10: Demosocratic media:

One of the main challenges in the world of today is the enormous control a few major media companies have over most of our both printed and digital media.

This started more than 100 years ago, and one of the first successful political media campaigns was to make the US take part in the first world war, which according to polls was absolutely unwanted by the majority of American citizens, but wanted by the American power establishment. Through a skillfully orchestrated media campaign, the US was made to enter first world war anyway. Today, a small minority of big media companies like Google and Facebook controls the digital media, and media conglomerates like Fox, Comcast, 21st Century Fox, Bertelsmann and Walt Disney owns a vast majority of the film and printed media.

Before the United States Senate Judiciary Subcommittee on the Constitution Tuesday, June 16, 2019, Dr. Robert Epstein (1), stated that "In 2016, biased search results generated by Google's search algorithm likely impacted undecided voters in a way that gave at least 2.6 million votes to Hillary Clinton (whom I supported). I know this because I preserved more than 13,000 election-related searches conducted by a diverse group of Americans on Google, Bing, and Yahoo in the weeks leading up to the election, and Google search results – which dominate search in the U.S. and worldwide – were significantly biased in favor of Secretary Clinton in all 10 positions on the first page of search results in both blue states and red states."

There are countless examples false media campaigns in the medical field, sponsored by the same people that own the medical industry, i.e. the enormous campaign for the Swine Flu vaccine and the coverup of its potential side effects.

The chief of the psychiatric department of WHO, Jules Angst, recently together with his co-workers, published a very well performed study showing that the one-term effects of treatment with antidepressants was negative, not positive, meaning that people taking antidepressants in order to treat their depression had a worse long-term outcome than people who did not take any medication at all, even corrected for all kinds of confounding factors. (2)

Why did this article not reach the headlines of mainstream media, when as much as 12-20 % of the American population take antidepressants? (3) This list can continue forever...

Recently, one of the most popular YouTube channels in Sweden, the government critical and medical industry YouTube channel "Swedish Webtelevision" was taken off YouTube without motivation or warning, without a doubt because of political reasons. After big protests, it was reinstalled again after a couple of days.

You can make your own experiment. Just try to write something, very well proven with references and everything into Wikipedia, that goes against the interests of mainstream medicine and Big Pharma, and it will most likely be deleted within five minutes.

In order to make Demosocracy work, it is of outmost importance to have access to free, unbiased scientific and documentary information. Create a publicly owned Media/Internet company governed by Demosocracy!

As we mentioned above, this company hopefully beat the Internet giants of today by competing in the free marketplace. The Internet infrastructure shall be considered a public domain, just like the roads of most countries and not be allowed to be controlled by private interests. All kinds of undue surveillance shall be strictly forbidden and Internet privacy shall be a human right.

Let news articles, movies and books be filtered without censorship according to different kinds of rating by using Liquid Democracy.

Today a small group of powerful people with vested interests mainly decides what is news and what is not news. Let democracy remove this filtering, and we will have a much more interesting and enlightening new media!

References Chapter 10

1. https://www.judiciary.senate.gov/download/epstein-testimony

2. Psychother Psychosom. 2018;87(3):181-183. doi: 10.1159/000488802. Epub 2018 Apr 20.

Antidepressant Use Prospectively Relates to a Poorer Long-Term Outcome of Depression: Results from a Prospective Community Cohort Study over 30 Years. Hengartner MP1, Angst J2, Rössler W2,

3. https://www.apa.org/monitor/2017/11/numbers

Illustration: https://pixabay.com/sv/illustrations/sociala-medier-hj%C3%A4lp-st%C3%B6d-finger-1432937/

Chapter 11: Demosocratic Medicine

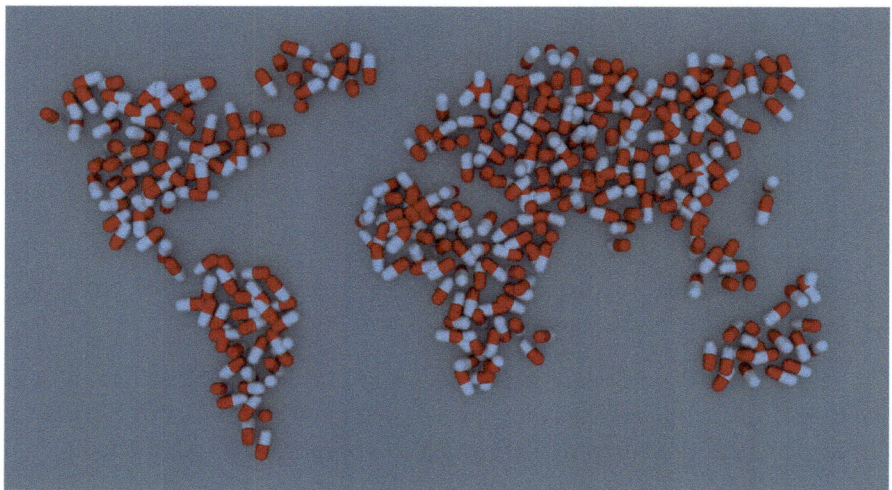

If someone finds a cheap natural cure for cancer without any side effect, it is very likely that he will not get any money to perform any research, because if the cure is cheap, it cannot be patented.

If he anyway manages to perform a few clinical studies, it will be hard form to get them published in a major so called peer reviewed paper, because these papers are dominated by the scientific establishment and the industry.

He will most get his articles published in a scientific paper that no-one will read.

If someone reads this publication, he is very likely to get into big trouble if he decides to follow the new facts and go astray from the official guidelines.

Because of these facts, we have still not solved the cancer issue, despite of billions of dollars spent on mainstream ideas.

I know at least three very promising, non-patentable cancer treatments that fulfill all these criteria. Psorinum 6x is a homeopathic medicine which stimulates the immune system to kill off cancer cells without any side effects.

There are at least five uncontrolled clinical studies from India showing amazing results on some of the most severe cancer forms like lung cancer, bowel cancer, esophagus cancer, liver cancer, gall bladder cancer and pancreatic cancer. His clinical data have been investigated by the US National Cancer institute in Bethesda, Maryland and published by ASCO, the American Society of Clinical Oncology

With conventional treatments, no-one survives five years with an inoperable pancreatic cancer in stage 3-4. Chatterjee had a five-year survival of 38%!

Despite that almost no-one knows about him, and last time we tried to contact him, we head he was in jail....(1-3)

Already in the 1960:s, Russian researchers did find cancer healing possibilities when people and laboratory animals reduced the deuterium content in drinking water and food.

In the late 1980:es Dr Gabor Somlayi in Budapest (4) started collecting and publishing preclinical and clinical data on treating cancer with deuterium reduction. He has now collected thousands of near miraculous cancer cases with a 2-7 times increased survival compared to historical data in most cancer types, and he still cannot get funding and access to the major universities. Water with a reduced deuterium content has been approved as medicine for cancer for dogs and cats, as the research and registration process are too costly...

In June of 2015, a well-respected Florida health practitioner, Dr. Jeffrey Bradstreet(5), went missing and was then discovered floating face down in a North Carolina river, a bullet hole in his chest.

Why would anyone order a hit on a generous family man who was just trying to do good? The death is still shrouded in mystery. Authorities almost immediately ruled his death a suicide, but his family says otherwise. Who shoots themselves in the chest to commit suicide, while positioned in just such a way that they will fall into a river?

Dr. Bradstreet's own son was brain damaged following an MMR vaccine at 12 months of age. The experience helped convince the doctor to look into a link between the vaccine and autism. He was working on two leading edge areas of medical inquiry.

First, he was doing research that seemed to support the compelling notion that certain vaccines could induce autism. He ended up testifying twice about this before Congress. Second, he was working with a new compound out of Switzerland that was greatly relieving, if not outright curing, cancer and other diseases. With vaccine revenues over $25 billion and cancer drugs over $100 billion, pharmaceutical industries risk losing huge profits if research like Bradstreet's continued positively and reached a wide audience. In fact, it could spell the end of numerous mega corporations.

Was there any evidence to document a financial motive?

Yes, just three days before his death, Bradstreet's research facility had been raided by U.S. government agents to shut down his research and halt his treatment of patients. The warrant that describes the items to be seized indicates a motive to protect pharmaceutical dominance and suppress natural cures.

What can we do to change this?

As we mentioned before, many medical issues are international, and cannot be solved on a national or regional level. Here are some suggestions for International Medical Reforms:

· Abolish Medical Patents, instead finance medical research through the world parliament, where all researchers can propose research projects which will be evaluated by and voted upon by the two chambers in the two world parliaments. Delegated voting will solve the problem with overload because of too many complicated issues. Medical research is clearly universal and a world issue.

· Let the world population take over all medical patent rights. Let the Pharma industry compete about who can produce and sell medicines for the cheapest prize.

· Make an open-source free software based electronic medical record system which makes every patient a research subject. The patients can partly write their own medical records by using intelligent questionnaires. They will also own their own medical data which they can decide to transfer to any therapist of choice, in any suitable language. This system will also provide data and follow up of all treatments, both synthetic and natural and provide data about what happens when you combine >10 different treatments, something which among our elders now is rather the rule than the exception. It will also allow input from life style factors, environmental factors, genetic and personality factors which will add a totally new dimension to medicine. The patient will of course decide himself which data he wants to share for the benefit of science, and how he will share it, i.e., with which degree of anonymity. As the patients will write most of their medical records themselves, this will also spare much time and energy for the physicians.

· The above-mentioned software system will also analyze the results of the different therapy methods, therapy method combinations and even the results of the different practitioners, which will make it easier for you to choose care intelligently.

· Make a universal medical publication system, where all entries will be accepted and evaluated by the participants, using Demsoocracy. All entries will be going through a sorting out phase, where the non-serious will end up in the public waste basket. Everyone can see every step, and if the main opinion disagree, publications can be readmitted from the waste basket. When a publication is deemed ready, it will be rated dependent on different criteria like public interest, scientific reliability, debated with votable pro- and con arguments and sorted together with similar articles according to the different criteria. By using this system, you can immediately find the most interesting and ground breaking research information. Every article should also have a summary in as plain language as possible. We have already started such a project on www.medicdebate.org.

· The above mentioned electronic medical record system will use results from the research publication and analysis system to always provide the practitioners with the latest available therapy recommendations and research results that are relevant to each patient. Difficult cases can be submitted anonymously to colleague's worldwide for advice and new creative input.

· Create an international Drug agency that is financed by the world parliament with no dependency whatsoever on the drug industry.

· Forbid medical advertisements. With the above-mentioned information system, good therapy methods, medicines and therapists will sell themselves. Medical results are more important than the wallet and marketing skills of the therapists and medical companies when choosing treatment.

· Create 10 000 Nobel Prizes in order to stimulate research and innovation.

· Lying in public by medical authorities should be considered misuse and abuse of their position and be equaled with perjury, and punished as such. If you don't know what you are talking about, please keep silent. This reform alone would change the development of medicine profoundly.

· Other necessary international reforms are abolition of software patents, agricultural patents, the disarmament of all national armies, the destruction of all kinds of heavy weapons including nuclear weapons, the creation of a sustainable world economic system without interest rates and with a minimum income guaranteed for every world citizen, effective environmental law,

We also propose a new scientific validation system called Independent Science.

We want to make an effort towards re-establishing the credibility of science by using the power of collective intelligence.

There is only one entity that can comprehend all the scientific information that is presented every day in the world, and that is everyone.

We strive to maximize transparency, democratic participation and competence in our decision-making process, and to minimize secrecy, administrative overhead and hierarchical power structures.

Therefore, we have created a website called www.medicdebate.org In this website, you can first read an article about a subject, written collectively in the style of Wikipedia, with direct links to all references provided within the website.

All information on this website shall be provided in three different levels:

1. The Plain language level, written so that everyone can understand, with links to the more advanced levels

2. The Professional level, written so that professionals can understand

3. The Scientific Paper level, written in scientific language, with Abstract, Methods, Results, Discussion and References.

In this website, every article and Medical Paper can be evaluated by using delegated voting, with possibilities to submit pro or con arguments that also can be evaluated and voted upon. These features are supposed to make it possible even for ordinary people to make an own standpoint even in the most complex scientific issues.

No information will be censured. The less good articles and references will simply be rated down, but not removed.

Evaluating science is therefore optimally carried out by using Demosocracy.

Demosocratic Research Funding

The next step is to create an interactive website, where donors to independent science can decide where they want the Independent Science foundation to spend its money. The idea is to let areas of particular interest be pin pointed through the www.independentscience.org website, and then give a possibility for researchers from all over the world to propose research projects, which could be funded by the Independent Science foundation.

Then the donors can give their support, or lack of support to the different by the use of an Internet Voting System. It has been shown form massive previous experience that you cannot trust the sound judgement of scientific professionals alone, as these people often have been subject to too much "brainwashing" or propaganda from the establishment, and in many cases are economically dependent on different vested interests for financing of their research. Going against the mainstream science cartel can also be risky for the involved experts, who might be scandalized in media, loose their academical positions and even be subject to violence and murder if they don't do the politically correct decisions.

Therefore, we also need to give these brave researcher legal support and financial compensation when needed. We also need to create an International tribunal against scientific corruption, that can use demososocratic justice to make verdicts and sanctions.

Who can we trust? Independent science can give you the answer.

I.e., there is massive evidence that there are many health risks with the introduction of wireless mobile phone radiation and vaccines. Another hot issue is the effects of carbon dioxide on the global climate, where some experts claim it is a massive effect, and other experts claim the effect is much lower.

This has resulted in a very polarized debate, with different pro and con websites

On our future website, we will present all these issues with the option of each side to claim their case using Demosocracy, so that we for example can have a page that as objective as possible presents the controversy, where after each side can present their pro- and con- arguments side by side, with the possibility for each argument to be voted upon.

This will give the independent reader an option to see both sides of every scientific argument, whereupon he/she can have a better possibility to make their own, objective judgement with the help of Demosocracy.

References chapter 11:

1. Chatterjee A, Biswas J, Chatterjee A, et al. Psorinum therapy in treating stomach, gall bladder, pancreatic, and liver cancers: A prospective clinical study. Evid Based Complement Alternat Med 2011;2011:724–743.

2. Chatterjee AK, Chatterjee A. Treatment of oral, lung, liver, gall bladder, pancreatic and stomach cancers through alter- native cancer treatment Psorinum therapy. Proceedings of the Office of Cancer

3. Chatterjee A, Bhattacharya S, Chatterjee AK, et al. A Phase-II single armed clinical trial involving an alternative cancer treatment psorinum therapy in treating non-small cell lung carcinoma (NSCLC). J Clin Oncol 2010;28(suppl):7s(abstract 2592). Complementary and Alternative Medicine of NCI: Cancer Researcher and CAM Practitioner Fostering Collaboration; Advancing the Science, October 22–23, 2007.

4. Deuterium depleted water effects on survival of lung cancer patients and expression of Kras, Bcl2, and Myc genes in mouse lung. Gyöngyi Z, Budán F, Szabo I, Ember I, Kiss I, Krempels K, Somlyai I, Somlyai G. Nutr Cancer. 2013;65(2):240-6. doi: 10.1080/01635581.2013.7565

5. http://www.thrivemovement.com/who-killing-healers-and-why

Illustration

https://pixabay.com/sv/illustrations/v%C3%A4rlden-karta-piller-jorden-1185076/

Chapter 12: Demosocratic Consciousness:

My daughter Maneka once went to a free boarding school in England, where there was no obligation for the students to take part in any classes, and the students were free to choose which classes they wanted to, and on which level.

This meant that there could be many different age groups in the same class and that the teachers had to make interesting lectures, otherwise no-one would attend. It was not only the teachers giving grades to the students but also the students giving grades to the teachers. The first thing you noted when visiting this school was how enthusiastic the children were about learning. I remember sitting down playing some piano in the school. The children immediately surrounded me, asking how they could do that too, wanting me to teach them how to play it. This school also had top grades in all subjects when compared to other schools in England, because of the great enthusiasm of the un-enslaved kids and teachers...

When the burden of enslavement is dropped, a great ocean of enthusiasm and creativity will be the result. You can say that the natural state of humans is to be enthusiastic, compassionate and loving, and when this condition is disturbed by slave consciousness, the result will be boredom and passivity.

This school did not allow any students to join that was over the age of 13, who had attended normal schools. The reason was that they usually could not handle freedom and be constructive. They would usually sabotage education for the other kids. Another exception was Japanese kids. They were normally brought up in a very authoritarian manner, which meant they would spend the first two weeks in school bowing and being polite. When they realized there was no-one to punish them or dictate what to do, they would end up somewhere in the trees, very rarely attending lessons, and often making havoc and disorder.

This is maybe a major issue in creating a new society. Not everyone will have the maturity and aliveness inside to be able to take part in this kind of lifestyle.

In order to succeed, such experiments need a strong peer group with good communication, free minds, and open emotional life, without the habit to suppress their peers.

Just a few dominating persons with a "master/slave mentally might be able to destroy the entire project, whether it's the setting up of a community, a co-operative project or a political party.

How to Exorcise the Master Demon

From the movie "Life of Brian", where the crowd demands to get a speech from their Messiah, Brian.

"BRIAN: Look. You've got it all wrong. You don't need to follow me. You don't need to follow anybody! You've got to think for yourselves. You're all individuals!

FOLLOWERS: Yes, we're all individuals!

BRIAN: You're all different!

FOLLOWERS: Yes, we are all different!

DENNIS: I'm not.

ARTHUR: Shhhh.

FOLLOWERS: Shh. Shhhh. Shh.

BRIAN: You've all got to work it out for yourselves!

FOLLOWERS: Yes! We've got to work it out for ourselves!

BRIAN: Exactly!

FOLLOWERS: Tell us more!

BRIAN: No! That's the point! Don't let anyone tell you what to do! Otherwise-- Ow! No!

Just a few dominating persons with a "master/slave mentally might be able to destroy the entire project, whether it's the setting up of a community, a co-operative project or a political party.

How can this problem be solved?

<u>Here are some suggestions:</u>

1. Make a personality test before recruiting people, where the master/slave minded can be sorted out from the enthusiasts.

2. Make rehabilitation programs for the retrieval of creativity and enthusiasm from the master/slave damaged people

3. As soon as you notice a conflict or bad feeling in the community, all activities should be stopped and the members shall try to analyze the cause of the conflict. It is of utmost importance to care of all these kind of disturbances ASAP, otherwise, they tend to build up to take away more and more of the positive energy from the group. You may use the list on page x with the different characteristics of master/slave versus egalitarian/creative personality types as a helpful tool in order to understand the problem. If someone displays too many master/slave personality traits too often, they have to attend a rehabilitation program, or in worst case abandon the project, otherwise the mental health and productivity of the entire group might be compromised.

This a summary of the differences between the authoritarian and Egalitarian/Demosocratic system characteristics:

Master/Slave:	Demosocratic:
Hierarchy	Flat organization
Elections to rule	Lottery or elections to serve
Elitism	Egality
Competition	Cooperation
Authoritarian Rule	Democracy
Corruption	Integrity
Them and us	We
Separation	Connection
Boring	Fun
Censorship	Freedom of speech
Domineering	Listening
Active Board members -Passive Crowd	Equal possibilities to participate
Bosses decide	Members decide
The power sees you	You see the power
Secrecy	Transparency and openness
Using rule techniques	Exposing rule techniques
Backstabs	Constructive confrontations
Grey and no humor	Colorful and artsy
Will to power	Will to freedom
Formalism	Love
Perfectionism	Tolerance and self-distance
Exclusion	Inclusion
You are not good enough	It is Ok to be who you are!
Falsehood and Manipulation	Truth and honesty
Condemnation	Acceptance
Judgmental	Forgiving
Taking attention	Giving attention
Destructive	Creative

Lose-lose	Win-win
Person-cult	<u>The</u> group and me first
Take	Give responsibly
Spreading propaganda	Spreading knowledge
Acting like you are God	Humbleness
Control need	Trust

The Master Demon in Samoa

I have always felt unable to identify myself with our western culture, religion, and mindset. In 1987 I made a tour to the South Pacific with my family in order to see if that could be a place for us to live. I had read many books about the paradise Islands in the Pacific by Thor Heyerdahl, Margaret Mead, and Erik Damman.

One book that made a particular impression on me was the book Tuiavii's Way : A South Sea Chief's Comments on Western Society"

The book is about the Samoan chief Tuaivii, who traveled to Europe at the turn of the 20th century and wrote a commentary condemning the very foundations of Western society, describing our impersonal, stressful, slave-like life and lack of happiness, very similar to our description in the beginning of this book describing the salve mentality.

Therefore, I decided to go with my family to Samoa in order to check out this place in reality. There were somethings that immediately caught my attention as soon as I arrived.

1. There was no private property or privacy. There weren't even walls in most houses. When taking the bus from the airport, you could watch straight into the houses, see people brushing their teeth, etc. There was also very little concept of private property. You could not buy land. Things were not really private, they somehow circulated. When I once spilled on my t-shirt during a ceremonial dinner with the chief and his tribe, I simply was given a new one, and they also expected meet share my property with them.

2. There was no stress. It was the first time in my life when I could really relax. When I took the ferry from the main Island Upolo to the bigger but less populated island, Savaii, everyone on the boat fell asleep within 10 minutes.

3. There was no concept of loneliness and social isolation. People had very strong social bonds and everyone was part of an extended family or Aiga, in which they shared all property and all land.

4. There was no concept of a career. They had some kind of hierarchy and were eager to obtain different titles that increased the prestige of the different tribal members. I order to obtain a chief title "Matai" it was important that you were a good public speaker who was generous and that you contributed a lot to the tribe, i.e. arranging great ceremonies, festivities, and sporting events. If someone used his ambition to build a house with a fence around that he did not share freely with his extended family, he would be considered crazy and become a social outcast. In the west, one of the first questions in a conversation with a new acquaintance uses to be "What is

your profession?". In Samoa, this never happens, at is does not really matter. They use to ask "What is your religion" instead, as this is the part were the master demon somehow has managed to get a small entrance in their souls through western religions and schooling, and the differs churches like the catholic church, the protestants, and the Mormons always compete about the attention of the Samoans.

The biggest downside with Samoa is that the islands have been visited by Christian missionaries who had inflicted many of our western thoughts about sin and sexual taboos, which in many ways had destroyed many of the more ancient traditions.

It was peaceful to sit in the open warm air with the chief and his extended family performing a traditional kava ceremony and share the warm friendliness and openness of the Samoan culture, and I have always been longing back to Samoa since then. I had never felt so relaxed and peaceful before in my entire life, and I believe that was because that the influence of the Samoan culture had made my slave demon partly disappear for a couple of days.

Unfortunately, I was not brave and mature enough in order to make my slave demon go away, and that very demon told I had to go back to Sweden in order to make money, pay back my bank loans etc.

Now, when I write this book, many of my old experiences and memories can be seen in a new light and I feel that everything I have been doing in my previous life has been a search for the wisdom that I finally have gathered in my old age by co-authoring this book.

I can see how I have been programmed by my schooling to always compete for the best grades, being the best musician and the best sports performer. How I never was good enough, although I was one of the highest performing and talented kids that I ever have heard about. (I was an elite volleyball player, an accomplished pianist, a philosophical and mathematical wonder kid and had highest degrees in all subjects in school) How I tried to compensate for my inner emptiness and loneliness and lack of connection with my true, peaceful self with the strive for wealth and recognition. I am although grateful for the fact that my parents never pressured to perform, and that they somehow respected my intelligence, freedom, and integrity more than most other parents, partly because they're so busy being creative themselves by inventing, playing music, reading philosophical and spiritual literature painting and sculpturing.

It was a bit lonely, but somehow, no-one managed to complete crackdown on my spiritual self-confidence. That created a little glitch between me and my master demon, and that is the reason why I am one of the co-authors of this book.

Most other people end up identifying with the master demon and lived almost their entire lives according to its commands.

It tells you to always be busy and that relaxation is a sin, that you must be rich and famous in order to be good enough, and even if you become a millionaire, you must become a billionaire, and if you are a billionaire, a trillionaire). There is always the greed for more money and recognition, and the fear of poverty and disdain.

If you are a sportsman, you must become the best in the world, if you are a musician, you must compete in music competitions, if you are a model, you must be more beautiful than the others. Even when you make love, you must be the perfect lover and be better than the others. You are never good enough, and in order to strive for more money and recognition, you don't have time to hang out with your friends and enjoy love and genuine friendship,

I can now clearly see how this demon has been taking away my happiness and have been torturing me and commanding me every single day of my life, except in a few good moments in Western Samoa, always thinking about what to do next, planning, arranging and worrying.

I now understand why I fell so deeply in love with my present wife Dina. She is a very intelligent woman, but also almost completely without unnecessary ambitions. She managed to make a career as medical doctor but has an excellent ability to relax and enjoy life when she is free from obligations. This gave me the resting place from my master demon that I longed for so much. She is a little piece of Samoa in my very home, although she also has some problems with her master-demon.

Many eastern mystics and western thinkers like Eckhardt Tolle call the master demon "The mind" and gives meditation lectures and different techniques on how to free yourself from it. I don't completely agree with this wording. The mind is an inherent part of ourselves that we need in order to analyze things, relate and survive, and without it, we cannot function. It is a natural part of all human beings and probably all animals as well. The mind is in my opinion a completely natural phenomenon. The master demon is in my view a much better concept.

This master demon is not necessary for analyzing, relating and for survival, and is the result of certain historic, political, religious and economic circumstances. When this phenomenon can be understood and analyzed, we can also have the possibility to find methods to free ourselves from its influence and create a new, better society, free from slavery and slave mentality.

References Chapter 12:

1. Tuiavii's Way : A South Sea Chief's Comments on Western Society Eric Scheuermann and Peter C. Cavelti Publisher: Legacy Editions; First English Edition edition (November 1997) ISBN-13: 978-096824690

Illustration: Samoa, own photo

Chapter 13: How can we step by step form our new society?

There are many things we can do in order to contribute to a slave-free society. One way is to work inside the current political system and create parties governed by Democracy, like Demoex thus using the current political system in order to create change.

This this can be possible but also requires a major shift in mentality and values in a democratic direction. It also requires that the constitutional rules within the party is locked to Demosocracy – otherwise non-understanding members or saboteurs from other parties of the party can sabotage the whole project.

Another way is to, if possible, refuse to contribute and pay taxes current system and instead spend your money and energy on a new system. One such project is called "The New Earth Project", initiated by the musician and philosopher Sacha Stone(1).

They want to create a new, slave free society by inspiring people to abandon the current system and create a new one by also using democratic principles, creating a new economic system based on crypto currencies, living in new earth communities and creating a new kind of holistic science.

Another way to create it is by using the capitalistic system: creating cooperatives operating with Demosocracy as much as possible to make sure the people own the market and thus controls the means of production. All that is necessary for this is:

- A decision making system for Demosocracy.

- An internal currency (for work done evaluated in relation to time-consumption and quality).

- Effective marketing

- Participants.

The internal currency can in the beginning be set towards some global currency in value.

Effective marketing can easily be achieved by having a lot of companies and a lot of workers spreading the ideas.

We need to meet in real life and form social bonds, this is something that our society does not want and makes sure those without technology ends up outside of the Demosocratic paradigm.

Capitalism is very inefficient in its core as it spends a lot of it profit on controlling the workers and feeding power addicted capitalists.

We need to live together, like the natural state of humanity – we need to go back to it. We need to devise dream-clubs where we help each other reach our dreams, each other's needs. We need to party together a lot. We need to live with our elders and our children. We can all cooperate without the need of some huge social-government agency or companies. The civil society needs to organize themselves, becoming the state, owning the companies, living in the naturally best way with the new technology, creating the transhumanist garden of Eden through Demosocracy and a loving, tolerant, creative and enthusiastic demosocratic consciousness.

References:

1. https://newearthproject.org/

Chapter 14: Freedom Town, a vision of a slave-free municipality.

In this chapter, we will make a vision of how a slave-free municipality can be manifested. In order to reach that goal, some precautions have to be taken.

Tribal life in a new version

Freedom Town will be organized in many small communities, with a maximum of 50-500 members in each tribe. Research has shown that most people cannot handle more than 100-150 close connections, and if the groups get bigger, they tend to become impersonal and needs to be divided into smaller groups. Of course, these tribes can co-operate in organizing bigger projects, but the core group should not exceed 500 people.

The tribe will take care of all basic activities like housing, getting food, social security, schooling, child-rearing and care for the elderly. There will be no need for kindergartens or elderly homes. Many tribes can together organize higher education facilities, factories, hospitals (if hospitals still will be needed) and other large-scale projects. Everyone will be born into a tribe, which means, belonging to a tribe will be a human right. If you want to move to another tribe in order to i.e. build a family with a new partner or relocate to another part of the world, you have to be adopted into that tribe. With this system, there will be no poverty, social isolation and lack of food, schooling, culture, and basic necessities anymore.

Within the tribe, all property is shared by the tribal members, just like in a family. Most of the decisions in the tribe will be made through face-to-face communication and in common physical meetings, but there will also be a Demosocracy software available to support an optimal decision-making structure.

Schooling and Child Rearing

The tribe will be responsible for child-rearing and basic schooling, meaning that every child will have many adult connections and inspiration sources. With the help of modern IT technology, much of the schooling can be made within the tribe, and there will be plenty of well known, loving adults to take care of the children if their parents need to go to work somewhere else or travel.

There will be no formal school with a school building, classes, and teachers, but a continuous learning process for everyone during the entire lifetime, encouraged by free knowledge exchange and lots of inspiriting education programs freely available on the Internet and education gatherings/conferences.

Every child will have the freedom to develop their own unique interests and study what turns them on while learning how to co-operate with others in a constructive way in order to create a functional living social organism together, where everyone is different and co-operates. There will be no need for competition, educational careers and search for power positions.

Taking care of the sick and the elderly

I once joined a lecture by the famous clown/doctor Patch Adams, who was portrayed in a major Hollywood movie by Robin Williams.

He asked the audience:" How many of you want to spend your last days in a nursing home?" No-one raised their hands.

Then he asked: "If no-one wants to spend his last days in a nursing home, why do we then have nursing homes?"

These things will be naturally taken care of by the tribe, which will be big enough to absorb all these needs without being overburdened, in contrast to a nuclear family, which is too small to be able to take care of i.e. a sick grandmother in the home. Therefore, there will be no need to pay tax for elderly care, schools, and kindergartens, and our children, sick and elders will be taken care of by loving relatives and friends, instead of impersonal slaves.

Work and Career

All work will be done in co-operative structures governed by the principles of Demosocracy, there will be no employees and no owners anymore, just independent, free individuals interacting freely together in order to create wealth, fun and prosperity.

Demosocratic Banking

There will be no banks anymore. All new projects will be funded by crowdfunding using Demosocracy. Allocation of resources and working power will be done by using Demosocracy. Instead of Fiat currency, everyone will use a time-based cryptocurrency that cannot be speculated upon and will guarantee free trade and fair financial transactions.

Demosocratic Medicine

There will be very little need for large scale hospitals any more, as the technology development in medicine will be geared to more and more affordable and usable high-tech devices for a low cost, in combination with expert systems available for all citizens.

The old paradigm of selling synthetic symptom reducing patentable drugs will be largely abandoned in favor of spreading a healthy lifestyle and curing diseases at its root with natural methods.

Resources for medical research will be allocated by using Demosocracy and all research results will be published online by using Demosocracy as a peer review and quality ratio system. There will be no fake results and publication bias anymore. Privately funded research will not be taken seriously, as it is a well-known fact that it cannot be relied upon. Medical patents will be replaced by a multitude of "Nobel prices" allocated and funded by the principles of Demosocracy, in order to replace the drive for creativity, formerly provided by medical patents.

Hospitals will be governed by co-operatives without any kind of hierarchical power structures and basic care will be taken care of by the tribes.

Demosocratic Justice

Experience shows that when well-being and democracy are empowered, criminality disappears. Switzerland has, for example, a very low rate of criminality. The need for a juridical system, with courts, jails, and punishment will most likely disappear, but in case some individuals create severe trouble for other members of their tribe, the tribe will decide how to address the problem. If the tribe cannot handle it alone, it can look for help from other tribes and maybe refer the troubled individuals to special rehabilitation programs sponsored by many tribes, where the disturb individuals can get special attention and optimized care, in combination with protecting society in an effective way from their violent or destructive habits.

Unlikely conflicts between different tribes and cooperatives can also be handled by using the so-called conflict solving forum described in chapter 11.

People Tribunals

Juridical conflicts and court cases can also as much as possible be handled by using Demosocracy, simply letting the involved community decide possible sanctions and actions in order to keep order and fight criminality at bay.

This can also be a very good way to spread Demosocracy, as very many people currently feel powerless and oppressed by the current corrupt society.

We will organize a website based on Demosocracy where everyone can file a complaint against corrupted bureaucrats and institutions that currently have the powering society. Then we collect support for the complaints and decide sanctions together. I believe this institution can be one of the most powerful change makers in the future.

Demosocratic Culture and Science

Everyone will become a scientist and renaissance man and will take part in scientific and cultural projects. There will be no copyright or patents any more as everyone will enjoy being creative in fellowship with others, there will be a good living standard and social security for everyone provided by the tribes. All information, culture, and science will be shared freely and sponsored by using demosocratic banking and resource allocation.

You are all invited

We invite you all to take part in this transformation of society, from an oppressive master/slave society to a free, tribal-based, egalitarian, Demosocracy-based society. Many might think we are radical, hippie-like dreamers, but we actually consider ourselves to be extremely conservative, aiming at redirecting society into the way mankind has been living for 99% of the time it has spent on this planet, but with the addition of modern technology, science, and Demosocracy!

More info about how to take part in this process and what you can do to enhance it will be available on www.unitedindividuals.org

Perhaps this sounds like populism – and indeed it is. It is populism with collective intelligence leading it, showing the path.

Now it is time for you to start working with the tribunal, fighting for Demosocracy and becoming an example of the future human.

Examples of what you can do:

1. Create a competent and user- friendly demosocratic software based on open source.

2. Start cooperatives, companies which are democratically owned and led.

3. Organize democracy within a party or start a democratic party.

4. Make sure that people start using Demosocracy locally.

5. Fight Corruption by using democratic people tribunals.

You have nothing to lose but your slavery and misery, and everything to gain!

Join us!